CAME HANES

Biography
Enduring hardship and outlasting challenges

Brandy S Cowen

TABLE OF CONTENTS

FOREWORD

CHAPTER 1: LIFE IS SUFFERING

CHAPTER 2: PUSHING ABOVE AVERAGE

CHAPTER 3: DIVING INTO A DEEP HOLE

CHAPTER 4: STRANGE AND UNEXPLORED TERRITORY

CHAPTER 5: DON'T LET THEM OUTWORK YOU

CHAPTER 6: OBSESSED OR AVERAGE

CHAPTER 7: RAMP IT UP

CHAPTER 8: BELIEVE TO ACHIEVE

CHAPTER 9: TRAIN HARD, HUNT EASY

CHAPTER 10: THE BEST NEVER REST

CHAPTER 11: THE FICKLE WINDS OF FATE

CHAPTER 12: LEGENDS NEVER DIE

CHAPTER 13: THE INVINCIBLE IMPOSTER

AFTERWORD

FOREWORD

Weakness follows every man. They're all of them.

I'm not necessarily referring to bodily weakness, such as being unable to move big objects. No, I'm referring to the true frailty: spiritual weakness.

Willpower flaw.

Inaction is the incapacity to act.

That is what a man consumes. Some may tell you they don't care, and they'll make convincing arguments about how much they like being lazy, but if you could be alone with them and offer them a pill that would give them an invincible spirit and an unwavering resolve to achieve, they'd all take it.

They're all of them.

Every single one of them.

Weakness follows us all.

We could have done more to erode away at your self-esteem. They take away your self-esteem and make you doubt your abilities.

We've all been in situations where we could have done more but didn't.

The actual skill of living a full life is to minimise the times when your inner bitch triumphs and to enhance your ability to rise and grind.

This is an art form.

Unfortunately, most of us do not approach our lives as if they were works of art.

The vast majority of us will leave this life as an unfinished canvas, a pale ghost of what we could have been if we had committed to conquering the mind and continually driving the body into action.

When we are motivated, we will exert some effort, but more often than not, we will find an excuse to nap and whine rather than pushing ourselves to perform beyond our comfort zone.

It is a very rare person who can lie down at the end of the day knowing they have done their absolute best, and an even rarer person who can do that consistently, day after day, year after year, until the days of laziness and self-pity are but a distant memory, drowned out by years and years of action and discipline.

There is an art to this, and my close friend Cameron Hanes is one of the modern masters of it.

A short glance at his Instagram feed would indicate a bowhunter who enjoys pushing weights and running trails to the uninitiated. To properly grasp Cam, however, a far more comprehensive and sustained study is required. He is a master of one of the least-appreciated art forms: the art of the maximised life. Layers upon layers of effort and discipline in this work offer a depth and texture to the life that is lost during a superficial glance by someone who doesn't know what they're looking at. It's an art form, with only those who are also out there grinding actually comprehending and appreciating how incredible this persistent work is.

On Instagram, look for the hashtag #keep hammering.

As of this writing, there are almost 449,000 posts, all of which are inspired by Cameron Hanes' way of life.

There are no days off in his universe. Days spent not improving are days lost.

The hammering never stops, and the inner bitch is never let to rest.

Many people speak in this manner.

Pretending to be a barbarian is, in reality, disgustingly frequent.

Many of these charlatans will post motivational quotes on social media and even give unsolicited advice on how to "chase your dreams" and "follow your goals," but my guess is that if you could randomly peek into their lives, you'd find most of these motherfuckers eating snacks and checking their posts for likes.

One of my favourite Cam Hanes quotes is "Nobody cares, work harder."

It's a fantastic statement for this day and age, when mature guys use beauty filters on their Instagram photos and everyone pretends they're extraordinary. Today's world makes it easier than ever to be full of shit. On the other hand, the beauty of this era is that when you come across someone who is actually, undeniably crushing life, you appreciate it like a hungry guy being fed a succulent elk steak.

I'm going to detail some of the things he does, and the list is so ridiculous that it appears to be nonsense.

He runs a marathon every day.

I once read that it takes six months for your body to properly recuperate after running a marathon. I'm not sure who wrote it, but someone needs to tell that stupid bitch that there's a guy in Oregon who works full-time for the Department of Water and Power and runs multiple marathons every week. He'll sometimes get up at 3 a.m. and run a complete marathon before work. Then he'll come home from work, practice archery, lift weights, and repeat the process the next morning.

He's completed several 100-mile events as well as several 200-mile races. These demand days and days of nonstop running. If you follow him on Instagram a few days after he returns from one of these self-imposed, soul-crushing torture sessions, you'll see him running or lifting weights with a big smile on his face.

Now, if you had told me 10 years ago that there was a guy out there doing all of this while working a full-time job and raising a family, I would have looked at you like someone who said their best buddy is Bigfoot.

Maybe I'd believe there's someone out there who can accomplish all of this, but I'd presume they're some science experiment being given performance-enhancing medications by a team of physicians monitoring his body around the clock to make sure he doesn't die from overexertion. But if you had told me that all of this was being done by some happy bowhunter working forty hours a week, I would have told you to get the fuck out of here with that crap.

It doesn't seem feasible, but it's true. What's more astounding is that he's managed to become the best bowhunter on the planet while doing all of this.

That's where the Cameron Hanes story becomes even more odd. His focus with physical performance is solely to ensure that he is at his peak for his true passion: mountain bowhunting for elk.

Hunting for wild elk with a bow in the highlands is an extremely difficult endeavour. The terrain is rough, and millions of years of evolution have honed the elk's senses to a razor's edge.

It takes getting within 100 yards of an animal that has spent its entire life evading mountain lions, bears, and wolves, and then releasing a flawless arrow into the animal's vitals under severe pressure.

Because of all of these circumstances, archery elk hunting success rates are relatively low. The average is roughly around 10%.

Even the most skilled hunters will frequently return home empty-handed.

Cameron Hanes, on the other hand, has won every archery hunt he's participated in over the last ten years. It's difficult to overstate how incredible that is.

His extreme commitment to fitness and manic pursuit of perfection in the mountains have made him the boogeyman for mountain elk, as well as a wonderful motivator to fellow hunters like me. There is no one else like him. A one-of-a-kind man with a solitary obsession: to be the finest bowhunter he can be. He has made his life into a masterpiece of concentration and focus, fueled by wild meat and superhuman discipline, and long after he is gone, when men sit around the campfire and tell hunting stories, his name will be mentioned with reverence and hushed tones.

I am delighted and honoured to count him among my closest friends.

—**Joe Rogan**
October 2020

CHAPTER 1:
LIFE IS SUFFERING

Running has always given me a sense of freedom. Despite the fact that I was in my mid-thirties when I ran my first marathon, I'd been running my entire life. I started school a year earlier than most children, and I can still see my five-year-old, first-grade self racing to school every day. A five-year-old pounding the pavement before school?

When I was in elementary school, there was a jogging contest in which we had a month to run as far as we could on our own time while keeping track of how many kilometres we had accrued. Every day, I arrived at the school early to sprint from fence to fence, which marked the school perimeter. Thirty-one repetitions equaled one mile. I ran twenty miles in the jogging contest my first year of doing this, in first grade, when I was six years old, and twenty-seven miles in second grade, when I was six years old. To break it down, there are approximately twenty school days per month, so as a five-year-old, my self-imposed objective was one mile per day before school; the following year, I wanted to do better. My mother saved the awards I received from the school for accomplishing this extra work on my own time.

"This demonstrates a willingness to exercise when it is not required," the certificate states. Every day, I came home and told my family how far I had run. I was working toward a goal and getting favourable feedback. In retrospect, I believe I was jogging to cope with my parents' divorce. And to make contact with a father who was no longer in my life. When I was a kid in Eugene, Oregon, the biggest legend was long-distance Olympic runner Steve Prefontaine, but for me, it was my father. In my opinion, Bob Hanes was Superman. My father excelled at track and field at Track Town, USA. He received a full-ride scholarship to the University of Oregon for gymnastics then, after failing out, a full ride to Oregon State for track, where he was expected to pole vault and high jump. He was around six feet tall in high school and could high-jump 6'4". My father performed the Western roll, in which the high jumper crosses the bar facing it and passes over it with his stomach facing down. He was friends with and competed against Dick Fosbury of Medford,

Oregon, who won the gold medal in the high jump at the 1968 Olympics in Mexico City. Dick devised a unique jumping technique that would be named after him during my father and Dick's high school years. High jumpers today perform the Fosbury Flop, jumping back first and kicking their legs up to clear the bar as they glide over. The track coaches approached my father and told him that if he performed the Fosbury Flop, he might potentially add a foot to his leap. If they were correct, he would have jumped 7'4". Fosbury's gold medal jump was 7'4¼", which was also a new Olympic record. My father never adjusted his jumping technique and never competed for Oregon State, where Fosbury eventually ended up and leaped in college. My father was more interested in partying than in being a serious athlete back then. He'd been obsessed with sports and being the best his entire life, so perhaps he was exhausted?

At South Eugene High School, Bob Hanes was a standout athlete. My father was the first inductee into South Eugene's athletic Hall of Fame, a school that boasted a plethora of amazing athletes. His classmates remembered him even years after he graduated. When our daughter was practising for the pole vault one day, two of her coaches approached me and inquired about Taryn.

"Is she Bob Hanes's granddaughter?"

I agreed by nodding. "Yeah. Bob was my father."

"You know—your dad was a legend around here," one of the coaches mentioned.

"Yeah, that's what I've heard."

When you grow up hearing about your father rather than meeting him, his legend just increases in your head.

He and my mother, Linda Brown, first met in South Eugene. I'll never forget what she said to me when I was five years old. "Your dad's legs are so muscular, they're as hard as this wood table," she added, indicating our oak coffee table. Small remarks like that made him appear larger than life.

Perhaps it was a blessing in disguise that my father did not receive more individual recognition in athletics, because he eventually became regarded as an incredible track coach at South Eugene. He coached long jump, triple jump, and pole vault state champions. My father had an impact on the lives of thousands of children during his thirty-year career. I continue to receive notes from youngsters he coached about how much of a wonderful effect he was in their lives.

Bob Hanes understood how difficult it could be to grow up and navigate life in general; his father died when he was three years old, shot in an alley in Seattle. He genuinely cared about the children he coached and delighted in assisting them in discovering what they were passionate about. And he had faith in them.

Before my father could become a great high school coach and inspire youngsters to win, he had to conquer his own personal battle.

Steve Prefontaine died in a car accident on May 30, 1975. Steve had won a 5,000-metre race earlier that evening at the University of Oregon's Hayward Field. He was only twenty-four at the time. Pre's Rock is named for the spot where he crashed on the twisting, narrow Skyline Boulevard.

Another car accident happened barely 10 minutes away from Pre's Rock four years ago. Nobody was killed, but it may have contributed to the disintegration of a family. It's one of my earliest memories of my parents' marriage. It's actually one of my sole memories. I was four years old when I awoke to the sound of my mother yelling. I went to find her standing at the garage door, yelling loudly and frantically to my father. When I approached her and followed her gaze, I noticed the side of my father's automobile was dented, as if he had just collided with another vehicle.

My father was an alcoholic, something I was unaware of at the time. Fortunately, Bob Hanes was able to walk away from the incident. My parents split shortly after. My father was involved in a following collision near railroad tracks and ended up in a coma for three days due to head injuries. Another close call.

My mother worked for the phone company, so she spent a lot of time in downtown Eugene. I'm wondering now if I started elementary school so early because my mom needed a break from me following the divorce, as I was frequently acting out. She was probably thinking, I've got to work, so get this kid out of my hair. He is able to begin school a year earlier than others. My elementary school was just up the hill from our house, so I walked there and back every day. I asked my mother about those days after writing this piece, and she said that beginning me early wasn't to give her a respite. She claimed I was a bright little guy who was ready for school.

Even while I enjoyed the jogging challenge I participated in in first and second grade, I had behavioural issues. Because my mother was at work, I was a "latchkey kid." Coming home from school by myself, letting myself in, and caring after myself till Mom returned from work later that evening. To keep myself occupied, I would usually commit harm. I once used a knife to cut the screen door screen, whacked a neighbour kid in the head with a fist-sized rock I tossed across East 39th Street, stole chocolates from the nearby Safeway, and so on. While the teacher was out of the room, I went up to the chalkboard and scrawled FUK in large, bold letters. This, along with other concerns, landed me on the "red light, green light" program. If I did well at school, they gave me a green light and a green card to take home, but if I misbehaved in class, they gave me a red light and sent me home with a red card. I can't remember how often I got a red card versus a green card, but it was a measurable thing. One thing has remained constant from then to now: I adore measurables. The green light might have indicated a nice day, but things did not improve. My mother began dating shortly after her divorce. Who could blame her? She was a stunning, green-eyed twenty something single mother of two boys. I despised her leaving on dates, and I despised the men she dated because they weren't my father. I couldn't believe she'd invited yet another man into our home. "Mom, I want it like it used to be," I recall saying. "It's just us and Dad." She eventually remarried, and my stepfather, Greg, joined the picture. I didn't like him, partly because he wasn't my father. They did, however, share one trait. They both had drinking problems, so he brought the same difficulties that had driven my father away with him. As I bounced back and forth between my parents, my childhood quickly became a never-ending race that I could never win.

I wanted to spend time with my father and gain his approval, but instead I got this stranger who appeared out of nowhere and told me how to live my life. He worked for a paving company and operated a roller, so he sat in the sun on hot asphalt all day, smoking cigarettes. Then he'd come home and drink, see me, and, in my thinking, plot something to screw with me. Here's the deal about my stepfather, Greg: He's as tough as shite. He grew up in a little hamlet in eastern Oregon, on a large ranch owned by his family. Ranching is tough work, so they were as tough as they come. Greg grew up with two brothers and two sisters, all rough farm kids who grew up to be harsh adults. Even after he got sober, he was a tough old bastard, running a 100-mile ultramarathon at the age of seventy. I may not have liked him for many years, but I have always admired his fortitude. And I'm wondering whether, in his opinion, being rough on me was an attempt to toughen me up for life. I'm used to tough love, but there was none in this situation. My stepfather always seemed to be in a terrible mood when I was a youngster. He was cruel whenever he drank, which was frequently. I once had to stack seven cords of wood, and after I was done, my stepdad believed they weren't piled well enough, so I'm fairly sure he knocked a portion of it over and told me to start over. He didn't work in the winter because pavement workers are frequently laid off and collect unemployment, so my stepdad was around more than either of us liked. We once had a bad fight in the kitchen that got physical.

There has to be a bad character in every movie, and mine was my stepfather. "Take the chicken scraps out," he said to me before school one morning.

"You take them out," I instructed. "You're going to be sitting here all day not doing anything."

We ended up on the kitchen floor, his veiny, dark-tanned arm around my neck. I most likely earned it. I didn't like him, thus I didn't respect him over those years. My stepfather wasn't a nasty person, but when you did stuff like this, you weren't going to get a favourable evaluation from your stepkid. When things got tough, I'd go live with my father, but that meant leaving my mother and younger brother behind. Pete is two and a half years younger than me, so when my parents separated, he was very small, and he didn't really know our father. He was more familiar with our stepfather, so when he started calling Greg "Dad," it was like a knife in my gut. "You're not doing that," I explained. I deeply hate that now, but I would beat Pete up simply to force him to see our father. I was constantly concerned about how my father felt. Pete had no relationship with our father, so it made logical for him to embrace our stepfather, but I wasn't about to. No, I told myself, I'm not going to accept this guy. All because I felt obligated to remain loyal to my father. Looking back, I would never put my children through something like this. Children should not be subjected to such nonsense. My childhood was horrible, and I had to put up with it. But, to be honest, I don't wish I had had a better childhood because it shaped who I am today. We all have difficulties, and those difficulties can shape who you are. It's all part of the adventure. Some of these difficulties arise from unexpected places and situations. You can't control the weather, therefore your life will be full of unexpected storms that will either break you, toughen you up, or simply teach you about the darker aspects of life that aren't depicted in Hallmark movies.

My mother worked with and became friends with this lady at the phone business when I was in the third and fourth grades. I recall her being incredibly kind and attractive. They went out on weekends, leaving Pete and me to look after the woman's teenage sons. My stepfather had a Harley, as did the husband of my mom's friend, so I imagine they went on road trips or maybe just out for the night. While it was a long time ago and I don't recall all the details, there are a few things I do remember that will likely haunt me for the rest of my life.

The adolescent brothers weren't the best babysitters. They took drugs and forced my brother and me to fight in front of their buddies. They'd yell and scream as if it were a game, instructing us on how to hit each other hard. When there was blood, the boys cried louder and became more enraged. Pete and I didn't enjoy it, but I don't recall having a choice, or it could have been a method for us young lads to get the approval of older males. The brothers kept an eye on us at our place since we had a pool table and they and their buddies needed something to do while acting crazy and getting drunk and high on those tense nights. They forced me to smoke marijuana so I wouldn't be able to tell them. We'd do anything they ordered, so I'd smoke marijuana and then they'd put shaving cream in my mouth to hide the smell of marijuana. The younger brother performed the majority of the contact with us and warned us that if we told on them, they would tell my mother that I smoked marijuana as well. I learnt then, if I hadn't before, that life isn't always going to be fun and lovely. My little eyes were exposed to the fact that there were individuals in this world you could never trust and who would hurt you for fun. Teenage guys already lack sympathy, but these two brothers went over and beyond. They once had me going so fast on a steel merry-go-round at the park that I jumped off, breaking my skull open on the pavement. My skull was split open and there was a lot of blood, but they forced me to tell my mother that I had fallen on my own. I believe I told her the truth in the end. I vividly remember them laughing at my blood-soaked blue-and-white striped shirt and saying, "Oh shit, your head is fucked up."

My mother didn't realise it at the time, and their mother probably didn't either, but the babysitting brothers were wicked in my eyes. I didn't inform my mother about anything they did to us until many years later. The older brother eventually overdosed on heroin and died in a Eugene park, while the younger brother took hallucinogenic mushrooms and murdered his best buddy with a knife when he was only fifteen. He was released from prison for that murder in his twenties since he was a minor, but he was involved in another murder and was sent back for several years. He's back out now. In middle school, I lived in Eugene with my father, while my brother lived in Marcola with his mother and stepfather. I really missed Pete. I used to cry all the time just thinking about my brother and how much I missed him. I had a paper route, so I got up at four a.m. to distribute papers. I had a lot of time to think when I was outdoors riding my bike in the freezing rain. During the summer, I would also pick strawberries and beans later in the morning for Evonuk's after I delivered papers. My goal was to earn 10 bucks every day selling BMX gear. During this phase of my life, when I had all the time in the world to think, one consistent thought came to mind.

This is terrible.

Happiness appeared to be an alien concept. The constant was pain.

Nothing about my middle school life stood out. I was in a bad mood. Even in terms of sports. Despite my competitive nature, I was not a natural athlete. Nothing has ever come easily. My father's genes didn't seem to have passed down to me, so I recognized I had to work hard at everything if I wanted to compete. Because my father was a great track athlete, I wanted to try to follow in his footsteps. I was pleased to see my stepmom, Kandy, come watch me at a track meet since I knew she was going to tell my dad how I did. He wasn't physically present, but his spirit loomed enormous as it usually did. It was difficult to get his attention in athletics while he was away with junior national teams. You couldn't do ordinary shit and expect to be appreciated. I knew I needed to make a statement, so I planned to do so in the 800-metre event at that meet. Our middle school district track meet was held at Springfield High School, which had a great rubber track and grandstands. I was dressed entirely in green, the colour of my middle school, the Hamlin Loggers. When the gun went off, I took off like it was a 200-metre sprint. I ran like Steve Prefontaine, going out hard and not giving up the lead. I raced at the front for a very short time, but at the conclusion of the first lap, I was dying. I still recall the winner of the race. Suiter, Greg. He was a natural track athlete who consistently won. He appeared to be a runner, tall and lean. I was the short-legged youngster who gasped at the finish line and finished last. I was relieved that my father had not joined my stepmother for this meeting. This was my usual. I simply didn't have it. That's how I was raised. Life has always been a struggle. Life has always been a grind, but perhaps it was more than that at this point. Maybe it was just plain agonising? Obviously, a parent's divorce is always difficult for children. What child doesn't want a mother and father to love them, ask them how their day went, guide them, and help them grow? That was not my existence. And when I was living with my father, he was never around because he was trying to keep his record business, Vintage Vinyl in Portland, afloat, and I was now separated from my brother. I only remember feeling lonely. Sad and distressed. So, yes... that was a slog. "'Why run?' is a question that is often asked," Steve Prefontaine wrote in a high school essay. "Why do you go out there every afternoon and beat your brains out?" What is the point of punishing oneself every day, of striving to be better, more efficient, and tougher?"

This was a question I began to ask myself—and was regularly asked by others—as I grew older. Prefontaine's response encapsulates his famed approach.

"The value is in learning about yourself." In this type of situation, all kinds of traits emerge—qualities you may not have noticed in yourself previously."

This might apply to completing a difficult race or enduring a traumatic childhood. Even in difficult circumstances, what do you learn about yourself?

I must acknowledge and thank my stepfather. He was the one who got me into hunting in the first place. The fact that my childhood hero was never a hunter is ironic. He had no desire to go hunting. My father used to mock me, saying, "Every time you kill an animal, you lose a brain cell." Of course, I know he was proud of my hunting successes. My father went to bookstores and convinced them to buy a half-dozen copies of my first hunting book, Bowhunting Trophy Blacktail. He loved and encouraged me, but he never hunted. My stepfather was the one who went hunting with my brother and myself. Maybe my mother persuaded him to "do something with the boys." The majority of rural people hunted. It was more of a casual hobby for some, and they certainly didn't practise for it like an athletic event back then. I was a bad hunting companion back then because I wore big-legged trousers that made a lot of noise as I walked. I was never silent. As we crawled along, my stepfather would be smoking a cigarette and getting irritated because we were making too much noise. As a result, I never liked hunting with him, although he did get me started when I was fifteen and my brother was twelve. I had to give it to my stepfather. He not only brought my brother and me hunting, but he also took us to this enormous deer hunting camp in eastern Oregon where his brothers went. I realise now how significant this event was. These mature males most likely did not want children around. I know I wouldn't have done it if I were them. When Pete and I arrived, I'm sure they were thinking to themselves, "What is this? "What the hell is a daycare?" They wanted to get together to hunt, drink, and play poker in the camp tent at night. My stepfather, on the other hand, bit the bullet and took us. He was responsible for my first deer kill. When I killed a young spike, my brother and I were alone. I was battered.I was shooting a 300 Savage with a cheap 4x scope when I saw horns, so I set the crosshairs behind the deer's shoulder and pounded the shot off from 150 yards. My brother glanced at me with surprise after I fired the gun.

"You shot a doe?"

"That wasn't a doe," I assured him, but I had second thoughts.

It's easy to perceive your childhood as a crutch rather than a chisel.

There are many divorces out there, which implies that many children come from broken households. "My family is so dysfunctional," I always hear people claim as an excuse for something. However, this is not a valid explanation because every family is dysfunctional in some manner. There are so many crutches individuals want to use to explain themselves, but in my opinion, you must eradicate each and every one of them. Get rid of all of them. Then persuade yourself that it's all up to you. What are your plans now that you've gotten rid of your crutches?

I could blame my drinking on a rough upbringing, but I don't. Blaming others is a convenient way out. It was all too simple to grow enraged when I saw my stepfather's drinking. But I could have easily had the same issue. Everything I do is excessive, so when I eventually started drinking as an adult, I went all in. I'd become really intoxicated. Nobody except myself could have blamed me if I hadn't straightened out my life. I know my father was an alcoholic as well, and it had a significant impact on my life. But I'm not flawless, so I can't pass judgement on him. He had a lot of potential that he never got to realise since he drank during his prime athletic career. Cancer took him in 2010 at the age of sixty-three, which seems very young for a cancer death. Who knows why he developed cancer after being sober and living a clean life for over thirty years? I believe he had a lot of regret, but that's just life and how it goes. He is the reason I am who I am today. Even though I didn't see dad as much as a kid because of the divorce and because he was so busy with his record store Vintage Vinyl, we became very close before he died, and I saw the influence he had on people. I always wanted to make him proud.

My father never lived up to his full athletic potential, but he set me on a path to do so.

I recently told my mother that I'm so pleased I went through all that garbage, being miserable, hating my step dad, and hating my life. I had the impression that I was never happy. I'm pleased I had to endure those storms. That's partly why I'm good at what I do now.

We are all raised to rely on others. Parents, siblings, friends, neighbours, and teachers. I didn't have anyone to lean on, so I had to do things for myself. If I didn't push myself—and there were times when I was quite content not to push myself—there was no one else to push me.

I discovered a true love and calling in bowhunting, and I found the ideal individual to drive me in that direction. But when Roy moved to Alaska, I had to decide whether to go hunting by myself or not because I couldn't find anyone who wanted to go with me. Of course, I went hunting by myself, and I felt at ease doing so because I had grown up being self-sufficient and independent. Not by choice, but because that's how life can be.

When it comes to exercising, I frequently hear the same excuses. "Yeah, I was lifting good, hard, in a groove, but then my partner's work schedule changed, so he couldn't make it." What is the significance of this? What does it matter? It's not about anyone else. It's all about you.

Being on my own toughened me up. It gave me independence and allowed me to become a skilled problem solver without having to rely on others. I had to use my imagination because no one else could, and I grew inventive and resilient as a result. My father's absence and my stepfather's hostility aided me in overcoming my mediocrity.

Of course, I had to go through high school first to understand how truly mediocre I was.

CHAPTER 2:
PUSHING ABOVE AVERAGE

Confidence is the first step toward success. Looking back on my life, I see an up-and-down journey, a never-ending effort to achieve "above average." The desire has been present since my first bowhunt, but there have always been murmurs of doubt about whether it's all worth it. There has been a bullseye on my back, being judged by everything I say and do, or is it just my own doubt that multiplies the negative energy thrown out there by others? Confidence is difficult to gain and simple to lose. It almost doesn't seem fair, but once you have confidence, you start working hard, and that's when you start to see success. As a freshman starting a new high school, I had no confidence and no track record to build on. When my father relocated to Portland, I decided to live with him. Suddenly, I found myself at a large school where I didn't want to be and where I didn't know anyone. My classes were difficult for me. As a freshman, I usually received Ds. I ate poorly and was inactive, so I gained weight, and to make matters worse, acne developed. When I was out of school, I would go on walks around Portland, near Burnside Street, with no money in my pocket, just to kill time. Some people go to the movies; I witnessed drunks stumbling around downtown, as well as people being assaulted and robbed at the bus stop one day. The most difficult aspect of that year was how much I missed my mother and brother. I wanted to return to them, but I didn't want to harm my father, and I despised my stepfather. On weekends, I took the Greyhound bus to Eugene to see my mother, and when the weekend was over, I stepped back on the bus and stared out the window, often with tears flowing down my cheeks on the way back to my father's. For various reasons, I wasn't genuinely pleased in either location. I quickly understood that something had to happen since the situation in Portland was dire. I made no effort to attend school or establish friends since I felt alone and alienated. I had all Ds in school and was overweight and insecure. So I returned to live with my mother for my sophomore, junior, and senior years. I knew it was hurting my father, but I was miserable and desperate.
After that, I went to Mohawk High School in Marcola. It was a small town with a modest school. Marcola was a logging town, and many

of the men worked in the woods. Growing up in a tiny town was wonderful, but like so many others from humble circumstances, I had low aspirations and no dreams. I wasn't looking ahead of me. The change of schools aided me since, while I never finished my homework and was not regarded as "smart," I was also not dumb. I started getting good grades. When I was a senior, I received straight A's. Sports not only provided an outlet for me, but they also provided me with direction. I played everything and was always in the starting lineup on my teams after I came back in shape and my feet beneath me. I was a wide receiver on our football team, and by my senior year, we were very excellent. I became the team's highest scorer, although that was primarily because we had a superb quarterback. Donnie Mannila and I were best friends at the time, and we lived three miles apart on Wendling Road, which was also the road where our high school was located. Every day during the summer, I rode my bike to his house, where I ran routes, caught ball after ball, lifted weights, and went to the swimming hole where we cursed the "flatlanders" (people from town). Donnie was one of Mohawk's all-time best athletes. All those days of him throwing me balls helped us form a strong bond, so he kept an eye out for me throughout games. Donnie, and especially his father, Don, put seeds inside of me for when I started running. His father was a fantastic runner who ran the 10K (6.2 miles) in under forty minutes. Donnie and I ran and raced against each other. We started calling it the Wendling Road Track Club. It wasn't long-distance running, and it paled in comparison to what I do now. It was simply something we did to get in shape for football. I realised I wanted to train hard in order to become the best athlete I could be. I enjoy being a part of a winning team, scoring touchdowns, and seeing the hard work Donnie and I put in over the summer come off. I too aspired to be a good student, but, like Donnie, I was never as excellent as he was in the Honor Society. Nobody was encouraging or pushing me. Nobody was staring me down and telling me I needed to perform better. I don't recall ever being questioned about my grades. I simply want to do better on my own. I learned to be self-sufficient as a result of my ups and downs in life. I was finally learning how to push myself. My mother was doing her best. I never had any doubts that she loved me. She had always liked me, but she had a lot going on in her life. She had remarried, was working, and was responsible for my half brother and half sister, Taylor and Megan. Of course, she had Pete and myself to contend with. I was used to being alone, so as long as I was with my brother, I didn't mind, even if we battled a lot over sports since we were so competitive. During this period, I found that I could inspire myself in sports. When I wasn't doing sports, I tried to keep as far away from my house as possible because there was usually a lot of tension if my stepdad was around. In the summer following my sophomore year, I found refuge at Grandma Heloise's house. On most days, in between playing catch, haying, and swimming, I would ride my ten-speed bike twenty miles to my grandmother's green house on 24th and Emerald in Eugene. My father's mother was Grandma Heloise. My father was up without a father since his father died when he was three years old, and my grandmother never remarried. She was a lovely and gentle schoolteacher who always looked out for me. Grandma Heloise always smiled when she saw me. She'd make me a plate of saltine crackers with peanut butter and I'd read a Stephen King novel as she played Mozart or Beethoven and read her favourite book while the grandfather clock ticked away the seconds. I spent a lot of time there, watched MTV, and then cycled the twenty miles home, only to do it all over again the next day. I have fond recollections of spending time with my grandmother, Heloise. Even though I wasn't particularly productive in her residence, I still biked forty kilometres per day. That was worthwhile because it assisted me in getting in shape. My father would occasionally stop by. He was still drinking at the time, so I simply went to Grandma's place. Hayward Field, the famous track-and-field stadium for the University of Oregon, was only a short distance from my grandmother's house. What was originally a cow meadow now hosts the most US Olympic Trials and NCAA Championships of any stadium in the country. I'd go over to Hayward Field whenever there were track meets and watch them through the fence that surrounded the field at the time, because I couldn't get in. There was also University Park, which I would visit. They had an outdoor basketball hoop where I used to play with other kids. We're playing some extremely good games. After my junior year of high school, I spent the summer working on my grandfather's ranch in eastern Oregon. Grandpa Bob, my mother's father, was a racehorse trainer who was tough as nails. This was a young man who moved out on his own at the age of fifteen, then joined the Army and served in Korea. Trust me when I tell you there was no babying when I worked for him. Papa taught me how to be tough as well as how to ride horses. I was a jockey boy because I warmed up his racehorses at the track before giving them to the jockey to race. It's difficult to restrain a racehorse. You can't be too huge because you don't want a racehorse to carry too much weight. I wasn't large, yet holding those horses required a lot of strength. Papa knew exactly what he was doing; his brilliance as a trainer was only equaled by his large personality and aggression. He was once named Oregon's quarter-horse trainer of the year. He was doing well, but it was primarily owing to his hard work and never-ending desire to win. Grandpa Bob taught me something else. Tomorrow is not assured, I was taught. My Nana, my mother's mother, drove up from their ranch in eastern Oregon on a Friday to pay me a visit and attend my homecoming football game. The Umatilla County Sheriff's Department called late Thursday night to inform us that Papa had perished in a vehicle accident. It was heartbreaking to hear this, because Grandpa Bob was a huge part of my adolescence. The following night's homecoming game was difficult to get through, but I played well and made some difficult catches. Papa taught me that every day, you have to give everything you have because the only thing that matters is winning. When a horse wins, the trainer, jockey, and family are invited to pose for a photo in the winner's circle. Anything less is considered a failure. By my senior year, I was enjoying teasing Mannila. I'd look at my hands and say, "These are the hands that are going to take us to state." Donnie and I got along well. But even back then, I could see some of the characteristics that have contributed to my hunting and training mindset, because I don't remember the catches the most. What I remember most about playing with Mannila is a pivotal drop.

"I'll never drop a pass." Famous last words I always used to say to my quarterback. I'll never forget my final game of my senior year. We were playing the Lowell Red Devils in a game that we would win 19-0, and I even scored a touchdown. But I also fumbled a two-point conversion attempt, my first of the season. I was the biggest baby on the sidelines, pouting because I fumbled a throw. My competitive personality was raising its ugly head.

I aspired to be the best even back then. After high school, I quickly realised that I was, at best, an average football player.

The term "average" has no definition in the Cam Hanes dictionary. My best work would not come from something involving a ball.
Are you good enough?
Along with Donnie, my college friends on the team included two guys from Portland named Keith and Joe, as well as Jeff Beathard. Bobby Beathard, Jeff's father, was the general manager of the Washington Redskins, and he arrived with some East Coast craziness. I thought I was good at wide receiver, but Jeff had the best football-catching hands I'd ever seen. The Los Angeles Rams selected him with the final choice in the 1988 NFL draft. After failing to make the team, I redshirted at Southern Oregon State, which meant I practised against the starting defence every day. On the field, there were clearly some animals. I was certainly not one of them. It was exciting, especially since there were some exceptional athletes on the field who went on to play in the NFL. The irony of college was that I never drank a single beer in high school. I was only concerned in athletics and grades. I knew I wasn't a great athlete, but I gave it my all because I wanted to impress my father. I discovered in Southern Oregon that even if I wasn't good enough to play collegiate football, I knew how to have a good time. I drank a lot of beer before returning to Eugene with my new "skill" mastered.

I basically messed about, sipping beer and not accomplishing much. I obtained work at a warehouse smashing cardboard boxes and baking them for $4.72 per hour. A job that a monkey might be able to do. After making large bales of cardboard, I stacked them with a forklift so that others could recycle them. The finest part of this work (perhaps the only pleasant part) was that it was where I met Tracey, my wife. Nothing in my life seemed strange or spectacular at the time. I didn't feel like I was squandering any talents or opportunities because I didn't believe I had any. It wasn't like I was disappointing anyone. Nobody anticipated much from Cameron Hanes, so I didn't expect much from myself.

My one and only focus in life—athletics—had abruptly vanished, and I was completely disoriented. Nothing was testing me. I couldn't think of anything I was excellent at other than being a smart-ass. I got myself into a lot of problems because of my words. People shape you during your upbringing, both positively and negatively. They look after you like Grandma Heloise or teach you like Grandpa Bob. They, like Donnie, challenge and motivate you. Family may provide an outlet, and friends may serve as motivators, but you must finally decide to dream. You are the only one who is pushing yourself.

Confidence can come from others, but it must be developed inside oneself. That needs time.

I was left wandering for a long after my Southern Oregon State experience, knowing I didn't have structured athletics to do anymore and recognizing this meant I had no true direction in life. Thankfully, Roy persisted in encouraging me to bowhunt, telling me that it was far superior to gun hunting, that there were fewer people, and that I would like it. Roy got me started, but the only way for me to gain confidence in anything was to do it. I soon concentrated my efforts on bowhunting. It was a challenge, just like athletics.

But this time, I had a different response to the age-old question of whether I was good enough.

Yeah, I'm good enough. In fact, I'm a lot more than that.

I discovered the ideal thing to work hard at, something that pushed me and that not everyone was brilliant at. When I was successful in bowhunting, it gave me a lot of confidence, and having confidence and positive reinforcement in anything was a strong spark for change in my life as a young man.

The truth is that I'm an ordinary guy who has had above-average bowhunting success over the last three decades. One thing is certain: if I can accomplish it, so can you. I started from scratch with no one pushing or believing in me. As a result, my tale demonstrates that even the most ordinary person may fulfil their wildest aspirations through bowhunting.

In bowhunting, confidence is everything. God's domain is the bowhunter's arena, and the only witnesses are the hunter and the hunted. There are no crowds to encourage you. You must be motivated by yourself. You have to be tough to experience success, and you don't get tough by thinking about it or postponing it. You must prepare for adversity.

You must believe in your ability to be tough.

CHAPTER 3:
DIVING INTO A DEEP HOLE

Two of life's most unsettling statements appear in the form of a question.
What if...
The older we get, the more likely it is that we will find ourselves saying these words. They can be used to express regret and disappointment. They can be wishful and desirable. They can also be filled with appreciation and relief in my situation. When I reflect back to those days after graduating from Southern Oregon State, I remember a young man who was aimless and adrift, feeling lost without athletics and assuming that this was how the rest of his life would be. I didn't see any signs on the side of the road cautioning me to drive with caution, advising me that I was approaching a dead end, or informing me that there was road work ahead. I ignored all of them. When you're drinking a beer while driving, it's difficult to observe those warning indicators.
What if I hadn't been fortunate? I might have perished.
Not everyone is so fortunate. I'm grateful for a second opportunity now. It just took a bit for me to grasp that it was a second opportunity.
When I became twenty-one, I thought it was fantastic that I could buy beer. I'd stop by Riverview Market on my way home from work and grab a six pack of tallboys. This is life, I reasoned. I can turn down a Coors Light. I'm suddenly a stud.
A stud who began to gain weight. Nobody seemed to mind. I wasn't meeting anyone's expectations. I was actually living down to them.
I would frequently drive to the Powerhouse, a swimming hole north of my hometown. I used to drive up to the side of the bridge, climb to the roof, and do a backflip, handspring, or swan dive into the river below. The Powerhouse was small and deep, with boulders on either side. It wouldn't have been good if I had gone too far either way, even if it was only a few feet. Hitting those rocks would have instantly killed anyone.
My friends and I arrived at the swimming hole to drink and do nothing. That was my existence. Nothing exciting was going on. This was life in a little town. Nobody believed they could ever change the

world. We were barely scraping by. There was no looking ahead or planning ahead. Nobody ever discussed what they may do in six months. We just inquired what we were going to do the next day. We were almost certain to be back at the Powerhouse, drinking and hanging out.

We all have habits. They can either be beneficial or harmful.

When Roy introduced me to bowhunting in 1989, he helped me change that monotony. Bending my first bow back and letting one arrow after another slip through my fingers was a start, a crack in my mediocrity. Killing my first bull after eighteen days of elk hunting was addictive, and I couldn't get enough of it. My soul was awakened by the challenge of the bowhunting woods. I was attracted to it. In the chase, my life had meaning, and I had a dream. My ambition was to become a backcountry bowhunter and eventually hunt more wild country than I had ever done before. But, as with hunting, it took time for me to break all of those bad habits and realise there was a better way to live.

I'd discovered my passion and purpose. I just needed to find the courage and perseverance to pursue it.

Giving up on a goal or abandoning a passion is the easiest thing to do in life. I understand.

I meet a lot of folks who are brand new to bowhunting. They buy a bow, go on a hunt, and realise it's just too difficult, so they give up. I see what you're saying.

The first year I went bowhunting, I missed sixteen deer. As a result, I've been there.

What if I had quit after the first year?

Wayne, Roy Roth, Dwayne Leavitt, Jeff Brooks, and I set out for Steens Mountain during bow season in 1991. We all climbed into two pickups laden with gear, pulling a trailer of llamas, preparing to tackle the Steens Mountain wilderness in southeast Oregon's rugged and gorgeous southeast. The mountain is located in Oregon's high desert and rises to about 9,700 feet. It was named for US Army Major Enoch Steen, who fought and drove the Paiute tribe off the mountain.

The country was harsh and vast, but on opening day, the bowhunting gods shined on me. I connected on my second hastily released but well-placed arrow after missing the biggest buck I'd ever seen with my first.

Because it was the biggest buck I'd ever seen on the ground, it had to be the biggest buck I'd ever killed. It happened not because of me or my ability, but because of one of my bowhunting brothers, Wayne, who invited me on the trip.

Not long after my Steens accomplishment with a genuine signature bow kill, I killed my biggest bull on another hunt in western Oregon's reprod. Consider me a youthful hunter with my $30 Jason PermaFocus binoculars, Fine Line sights, freshly double-dipped orange and white XX75s, and Oregon Valiant Crusader III DX bow. I'd attached two bear claws from the first bear I'd ever arrowed to the hood of my quiver. I also rubber-cemented a metal six-by-six bull elk head silhouette in between those bear claws.

My quartering-away shot from 35 yards was fantastic. The arrow entered at the last rib and exited on the far side shoulder, which meant I only had one hole (the entrance) through which to leave blood. Thunderhead 125s were used, which are solid, robust heads that performed the job. Even though I had a meagre blood trail to follow, that one flawless arrow took the bull down swiftly. The Roosevelt bull, on the other hand, was a large-bodied beast with hefty hooves that badly scarred the fragile earth. I followed his fresh, deep-cutting tracks down the hill for fifty yards before ripping back a wet fir limb to expose the fallen beast in a tangle of fireweed.

This five-by-five with black antlers was my best bull to date.

I recall every detail of these hunts like it was yesterday. As a result, the saying "The beast is dead." "Long live the great beast."

Bowhunting has infiltrated my soul. I had no concept how it would end up directing my every step through life's path at the moment.

Despite my advancement and success in bowhunting, I was still going nowhere in life. I was twenty-two or twenty-three years old, living with four men, and we were always drinking beer. My roommate received two DUIs in three weeks, both while driving my truck. I'm pleased I wasn't driving at the time, although it was more luck than smart judgement. I just didn't get caught. I wasn't living healthily and lacked a strong feeling of purpose. I wasn't responsible for anything or to anyone. I was constantly shaky.

When I crashed my truck while drinking one night, it served as a wake-up call. I was going too quickly and flipped the car, rolling it. The roof had been smashed all the way down to the seat's top. The truck had been totaled. Of course, I had forgotten everything.

I may easily have died or killed someone. There was no police report because this was a rural region and the police were rarely present. Wrecked autos were constantly abandoned in the ditch. We just contacted a tow truck, and it was taken to a wrecking yard.

Did I awaken? No. No, not yet.

Is there a link between my walking away from the crash and my father walking away from his? Was I following in his drunken footsteps?

My life had devolved into simply partying with a group of guys. Basically, I work during the week and spend my weekends either going to clubs or drinking at home or at the lake.

It wasn't an easy existence.

I felt I was a lucky bastard to have survived the crash, but no...

Cam, you're a complete jerk, and this time you got lucky.

You have not received a DUI. Yet.

You have not harmed yourself or anyone else. No, not yet. Sure, you got punched for being a jerk and intoxicated. You've had fights, even with friends.

You're a moron.

You're a jerk.

What if I had died that night? A wannabe athlete, young and stupid, choosing drink over life would have meant foregoing the opportunity to bring three magnificent people into this world. It would have meant giving up a great wife, profound brotherhoods, incredible memories, and incredible experiences. There would have been no Keep Hammering lifestyle if I had perished as a result of getting hammered. I would not have gone through the painful loss of my father and closest friend if it hadn't been for the heartbreak that revealed my own existence and purpose.

No one believed in me or was astonished when I smashed my truck while driving drunk. I walked away with only scratches and, of course, another chance to change my life. Thank goodness I did eventually.

After becoming obsessed with bowhunting, I decided to drop out of college.

Was that wise? No.

Would you do something like that? Most likely not.

People said I was fortunate. People said they heard I shot a raghorn five-point elk with a crossbow or a rifle, which would have been banned in my second year of hunting. People like him began fabricating stories to disparage my achievements. My first experience with hater envy. I didn't like it, but I couldn't change it.

This sparked a lot of rage after I killed the nice five-by-five Roosie and the enormous mule deer. Someone stabbed my eyes out with a tack in my photos at the Bow Rack. It didn't make a difference.

Weak people despite success. I simply kept hammering. I have to set a good example. Every parent wishes for their children to have more than they did. To lead a better life than they did. My father was not present, and I remembered all the times I wished for him and wanted to see him. I desired to be present for my children. I didn't want to die in a drunk driving accident, nor did I want to ruin a family by drinking. Every man and woman has flaws in their defences. I've uncovered my flaws and am aware of what's going on in my thoughts and emotions over the years. I knew the truth even back then. I couldn't deceive myself.

Alcohol was lethal.

I'd seen what booze did to my father, ruining what could have been something amazing, and now I was witnessing it do the same to me. As a result, I stopped drinking. Who knows what might have occurred if I had continued to live that way?

What if ...

One thing is certain. Nobody would want to read a novel about an alcoholic who lives in Marcola. I could easily stay there still, drinking the days away and sleeping without a single dream.

Alcohol was not going to aid me in any aspect of my life, particularly my hunting. I'm not passing judgement on anyone else, but I had to stop drinking.

You must be aware of your own talents and flaws. You must be brutally honest with yourself at times. Then you must put forth the effort.

Failure does not always mean that your fate is sealed.

When I returned from a year of redshirting at Southern Oregon State, I was adrift without sports. But what if I had pursued my ambition of playing collegiate football? What if I had been able to afford to stay at university and keep trying? What if someone was there to encourage or financially support my ambitions and dreams?

Every day, we wake up with a hundred what-ifs. They are intriguing to consider, but they are in the past. It's more necessary to consider what-if scenarios in the future.

As my involvement in bowhunting grew, I began to ask myself new questions.

What if we ignored what people think about hunters?

What if we abandoned prejudices and semantics about them?

What if we created the perfect predator? What would that entail?

It reminded me of a professional athlete, someone who was concerned with nutrition and who worked hard. Someone who desired to tear down mental barriers in order to become stronger than they had ever been.

I'm thankful for second chances and for gradually evolving from the person who jumped off the bonnet of his truck into some deep, boulder-lined swimming hole when buzzed. I'm glad I made those modifications. Every day, I'm thankful for my children, Tanner, Truett, and Taryn. They will, I believe, have a positive impact on the planet.

Take my word for it. Don't want your friends and family to look back on your life and wonder, "What if?"

CHAPTER 4:
STRANGE AND UNEXPLORED TERRITORY

It has been said that life has two pathways, one easy and one difficult. When Roy and I first entered the forbidding refuge of the Eagle Cap Wilderness and saw the awe-inspiring Wallowa Mountains in northern Oregon, it was clear that we had chosen the latter. We were constantly attracted to the more difficult path. Harder was always better for us.

I became hooked on bowhunting after my first elk hunt in Oregon's largest designated wilderness region, the Eagle Cap Wilderness, which spans 1,800 square miles. With its granite crags and unfathomable canyons, this rocky land was without a doubt Oregon's hardest. Bighorn sheep, mountain goats, mule deer, bear, cougars, and Rocky Mountain elk were just a few of the large game creatures that lived there. Many bull elk frequented this area without being harassed by humans. There is something amazing about a wild and rugged country, but it cannot be explained. I've been trying for decades. If you have the stubborn traits of the wild in your soul, you know. If they aren't, no words will change it.

When Roy and I arrived at the trailhead, we were 400 miles from home. This was significant since Roy and I had done 99 percent of our hunting within twenty minutes of our western Oregon homes before this trip. To put it simply, we were far over our heads.

Arriving here was a voyage in and of itself. We usually bought gas for our trucks five dollars at a time, but we didn't have enough money to get to "The Caps," in the state's far northeast corner. Roy eventually sold a collector's edition.His grandfather had given him a 30-30 rifle for $300 to use for petrol money. We couldn't afford to hire a horse packer, so we persuaded Roy's father to buy two pack llamas to carry some of our luggage into the Eagle Caps.

We had to make sacrifices in order to reach the woods, and the journey ahead appeared frightening and perilous. Where the heart goes, the body will follow, so Roy and I devised a plan to get into the woods.

Did we know if there would be a payoff, a payout, or if anything would be accomplished on this trip? Of course not, but we were still there. If you really want something, you will find a way to make it happen.

Roy and I wanted to live on the edge of things. We were in this vast wilderness to be wild and free, to seek adventure. This was our sole objective.

This is where Roy and I learnt the most important things about bowhunting. Finally, it's about life.

Bowhunting in general is difficult. There are many strong men who do it. But it's not going to be easy. Even the hardest man can be broken by the mountains. Roy Roth was the most rugged man I'd ever met or seen in the mountains. Without a doubt. Roy was the fiercest bowhunter I'd ever seen, with the finest attitude. I learned a lot from him. He is a significant part of why I am who I am today.

Roy was always good in the woods when I was a youngster. He could always beat the rest of us to the better fishing spots. He was dubbed "Gazelle Roy" because he was large but moved like a gazelle. He was a fantastic athlete who excelled in both football and baseball, particularly third base. We bonded and hit it off the moment Roy suggested I start bowhunting. We started hunting together and instantly clicked because we both had no limitations on how much agony we were willing to endure in order to achieve success.

Roy's father owned a construction company, so Roy worked for Roth Construction, and I worked for them for a period after graduating high school. We would usually work pretty hard in the morning and then leave early to go shoot something—carp in the summer, which we would then use for bear baiting. We both grew infatuated with archery and bowhunting rapidly and pushed one other to achieve more.

"Has a man ever done it?" This is what Roy and I discussed. We reasoned that if a man had done it before—any guy, ever—we could do it too. If a man had never done it, there was a chance we'd fail, but we'd try our hardest anyhow. We sought to push the boundaries of what was possible. That's why we drove eight hours to this remote area of eastern Oregon. We knew the hunting was better, the land was wilder, and there were less people out there simply because it was so tough, which made the wilderness with all its unknowns look like a giant piece of candy, and we were youngsters with an insatiable sweet tooth. Here's another of Roy's many demonstrations of toughness.

We trained llamas to tote our gear shortly after Roy's father purchased them. Roy was making some food on a single-burner gas stove with the llamas during one scouting trip deep into Oregon's Three Sisters Wilderness, using a saucepan with a handle that hung down on the bottom side of the pot, essentially right in the propane flame. We were heating water to prepare some mac & cheese, so Roy cautiously lifted the handle and grasped it to take the pot off the flame. As Roy began to lift the pot, the handle melted the flesh on his fingers since it was branding-iron hot.

Most people would have dropped the pot right away, but Roy couldn't since boiling water is a valuable commodity in the backcountry. So he laid it down as quickly as he could, saying, "Jiminy Christmas, that is hot." Roy didn't cuss back then, and in all my years knowing him, I never heard him say a single cuss word.

Roy had significant burns, seemingly to the bone, on the bend of a couple fingers' second knuckles where the pot handle had rested as he lifted the pot. After that, we stayed in the bush for a few days, and he never mentioned it again. He simply wrapped his fingers in duct tape and kept going.

Roy was the one. We both enjoyed bowhunting since it provided more adventure. There were more opportunities because the seasons were longer. Because it was so difficult, there were less people to deal with.

Mountains are nature's great equaliser. Roy and I believed this, so we sought out more rugged terrain than anybody else, thinking that it would give us an advantage in the real world, where those with money or connections had an advantage over regular guys like us. But in the mountains, material success, money, and fame are meaningless.

The mountains are unconcerned.

Your toughness and physical fitness provide you cash on the mountain. We realised that the harsher we were, the more successful we were.

However, the mountain always had the upper hand.

I've long concluded that individuals I most admire are those who live in the mountains. In my opinion, their determination, confidence, and spirit are admirable. One such person is Billy Cruise, whom most people have never heard of. For years, I was inspired by the renowned Billy Cruise.

Roy and I came across a large outfitter's camp five kilometres from our designated Eagle Cap Wilderness entry-point trailhead. We kept going because we had come here purely to be away from other hunters, and we eventually wound up fifteen miles from the trailhead, at the bottom of a massive canyon. We met a long-time wilderness bowhunter, a dentist from Eugene, Oregon, at this point.

"Do you guys need some help?" the man said, his gaze drawn to us and our frayed packstring.

"We've been walking all day and are just looking for some good elk country away from other hunters," I blurted out.

The dentist then told us a life-changing story about a man named Billy Cruise, an Oregon elk-hunting legend and the founder of the Oregon Bow Company, which made the bow I was holding. Billy had perished in an aircraft crash while searching for elk a few years before, but his legacy lingered on, especially for Roy and me, two young, eager bowhunters. Billy and the dentist have been to numerous camps together.

"Most of the guys in our party hunted within a few miles of camp, but Billy would head to the deepest and nastiest country in the Eagle Cap," claimed the orthodontist. "Every year, after dark, we'd all be sitting around camp, eating dinner or playing cards, when Billy would burst into the tent and roll a couple of bloody elk ivories onto the table." He'd then tell how he arrowed another enormous wilderness bull and packed it out of a terrible hole.

"I could tell you guys where Billy hunted," said the dentist. "No one goes there." It's too rugged for horses, and it's too steep for hiking. You're more than welcome to give it a shot."

"Perfect!" we said. "We just want to get away from people."

"You won't see a soul," said the dentist.

Roy and I tried not to look back as we walked down the trail. We tried to keep our cool and hide the wide grins that were tattooed across our grimy features. That dentist has just revealed the key to happiness to us. We'd never met Billy Cruise, but walking in his footsteps had given us a new lease on life. We were twenty-one miles from the trailhead and our truck after a final 4,000-foot steep ascent. We didn't mind. We were only concerned with the present. We were on a difficult path toward the unknown. Steve Prefontaine once commented after a race during his freshman year at the University of Oregon, "I've never been here before." It was uncharted territory. It's peculiar. You've arrived at a point in time you've never experienced before, and you're not sure if you'll make it. But I'm continuously discovering new things about myself. I haven't yet crossed the line into oblivion. Perhaps I never will."

Roy and I were exploring weird, uncharted, and exciting territory. I arrowed a lonely spike, my first wilderness bull, after several days and several close calls with some extremely huge bulls in terrain every bit as awful as the dentist had predicted. The insanely long pack out did little to dampen our spirits. It was in our blood to go backcountry hunting. The dentist was correct. We didn't see another person. Even now, many years, hunts, and bulls later, I have yet to see another human back there.

Why am I drawn to do things like this?

I finished the Western States Endurance Run, a 100-mile run over California's Sierra Nevada mountains, several years after first hunting in the Eagle Cap Wilderness. I finished in 22 hours and 41 minutes. Several times during the marathon, I questioned why I was drawn to activities like running a 100-mile race.

I believe it stems from the fear I felt as a young, solo adventurer hunting Eagle Cap. It appeared enormous and overwhelming to me, an inexperienced teenage bowhunter. If the truth were known, it would be terrifying.

I've had a strange thought since running my first marathon a few years back.

What if I could run across the entire Eagle Cap? Through the rivers and creeks, up the drainages, and over the mountains.

If I could do that, I could do anything.

When the day arrived when I could actually achieve that, it gave me the confidence to face all of my doubts and worries and overcome them, no matter what hurdles stood in my way. But it takes time to accomplish that.

Dr. Saxton Pope's Hunting with the Bow and Arrow is one of my all-time favourite books. It was written in 1923 and tells the story of Pope and his companion Art Young. "We also began preparing ourselves for the contest," it says on page 181. Despite being in generally decent physical shape, we underwent specific training for the major event." He and Young were prepared for a grizzly bow hunt in this case. He goes on to say, "By running, the use of dumbbells and other gymnastic practices, we strengthened our muscles and increased our endurance." On page 206, he writes on the difficult backcountry hunt, "We were there to win and nothing else mattered," later adding, "We were trained down to rawhide and sinew, keyed to alertness and ready for any emergency."

When I was younger and more inexperienced, I quickly discarded those few phrases. However, lines like "trained down to rawhide and sinew" grew on me with time. That was some tough stuff. If Pope and Young recognized the benefits of being healthy in the 1920s, I'm sure many other bowhunters did as well. The better shape I became in the beginning, the smaller the Eagle Cap Wilderness seemed to me. And it now appears to be manageable. In fact, even the most difficult mountains now feel familiar to me. It's where I feel the most at ease.

Roy and I were both lured to the mountains by the danger and excitement of the hunt. When I'm hunting or jogging in the mountains, I never feel more capable or stronger. It's as if I'm unstoppable. I'm capable of doing anything. Roy felt the same way about hunting in the wilderness.

The intensity and purity of life at high elevations comes with an underlying risk for those drawn to the wild. Because guys are all mortal. The mountains can be as brutal as they are beautiful, which is what pulled Roy and myself in like moths to a flame. This dichotomy meant everything to us. What's the purpose if you don't have it?

I knew from the start that what we did was fraught with danger. That was part of the agreement. Perhaps the finest part?

CHAPTER 5:
DON'T LET THEM OUTWORK YOU

I stared out over the lonely wilderness, firmly gripping my bow and feeling the weight of my pack, and there, laden down next to me, was the trophy of a lifetime. Some people wish to be wealthy or famous, or to play in the Super Bowl in front of millions of fans who celebrate their every move. In contrast, this is what I had hoped for.

There was no one cheering. The wind, sliding shale, and rolling rocks were the only sounds I could hear. Roy was the only thing missing from this hunt. I thought about that hunt every day of the year after our initial exploits in Eagle Cap. Now I was back, and I had won yet again. The only issue was that my partner had relocated to Alaska. I was embarking on what would become an annual solitary journey for me. Roy had assisted the pastor of his church in relocating to Alaska. Roy felt he needed to relocate north after driving across Canada and back. It felt like a divine calling. He was eventually recruited by a large construction company up there, so he relocated his family to Alaska. Roy was quite knowledgeable about the construction industry, and he finally launched his own company and became a very successful general contractor. Roy effectively took over his father's company, Roth Construction. They collaborated, but Roy rose from understudy to showrunner.

The only difficulty was that I had now lost a kindred spirit back in Oregon. I attempted to persuade others to go hunting with me, but the few who agreed only went once. That's all there is to it. The stillness, the vastness of the landscape. Others found it too much. Nobody else cared about it the way I did. That's how Roy wanted it. I desperately tried to locate another partner who shared my love of the outdoors, but I couldn't find a single one. You can't make someone like backcountry bowhunting. You either adore it or despise it. There is no in-between.

When I realised I was wasting my time trying to persuade people to feel the same way I felt about the wilderness, I had to make a choice. I had to decide whether to go by myself or not go at all because I couldn't find anyone who wanted to join me. Of course, I elected to continue. I made the decision that I couldn't rely on anyone but myself. I was once again compelled to push myself and travel alone. That was not my first option, but that is how life sometimes works.

For the next twelve years, I spent most of my time hunting alone in the vast and brutal Eagle Cap Wilderness. My entire life seemed to revolve around preparing for just one shot at the wilderness bulls and bucks Billy Cruise had hunted.

The wilderness is difficult. It will put you to the test and make you wonder how much you really want to be back there. This was the beginning of a rewarding wilderness experience for me. On those single quests, I discovered more about myself than I could have in a lifetime in the real world. Maybe it's because those hunts taught me how to bleed.

Bowhunting is not like other sports in that it requires a high level of running speed, agility, strength, and coordination. Anyone who is dedicated to doing their best and respecting their quarry, the country, and the time-honoured pursuit of bowhunting can achieve great success. I can tell you from personal experience that it all comes down to how badly you want it. Are you prepared to bleed? In most circumstances, some blood is required to fulfil your objectives. Many bowhunters, in fact, are unwilling to bleed. Isn't bowhunting just a nice hobby? A fantastic way to pass the time. A way to get some fresh air, go on vacation, and possibly even put meat on the table. I agree with what you said, yet it doesn't motivate me. The test is what drives me the most.

I was drawn deep into the most wild and inaccessible territory I could discover from the beginning of my backcountry bowhunting experience. I always wanted to be further in than anybody else so that I could hunt animals without being bothered. Perhaps there was a latent urge inside of me, a desire to test the boundaries of my own mind and self-imposed limits of what's possible?

What I immediately discovered was that the harder you push, the more people you leave behind.

The further you travel, the fewer people will be willing to accompany you. They resign for two reasons: they can't take it or they don't want to.

Will you keep going, even if you have to do it alone?

The vast majority will not.

I figured that if I could get back into the forest, I'd be able to find better hunting. If I was in better shape, I could get away from the other hunters. And I could outlast anyone if I was mentally stronger.

After Roy and his family relocated to Alaska, getting anyone to join me on a wilderness hunt was a hopeless struggle. I couldn't figure out why no one wanted to leave town after work on Friday, drive all night, hike all day in the bush for what amounted to a one-day weekend hunt, and then do it all over again to come back to town late Sunday night or early Monday morning just before work. It seemed like the best weekend ever to me. However, everyone is unique and has various interests, requirements, and priorities. My objectives and goals were absolutely clear.

As a result, I frequently drove and hunted alone. The option was to go alone or not go at all.

The woods tested me more mentally than anything else. The mind is powerful, and it can create problems that aren't even there, since we can obsess about things in a distraction-free country. Sleeping alone in the mountains is no longer natural for humans. We are taught to fear the dark, to believe that there is power in numbers, and to appreciate and become soothed by the comforts of home.

In the harsh, merciless landscape, I learnt to conquer my own self-doubt. I learned how to address my most prevalent worries. Meeting them impacted my life forever.

Since I couldn't afford premium hunts and never drew any highly regarded tags in the beginning, I found that the secluded location of the wilderness gave some incredible possibilities while also weeding out 99 percent of other hunters, as it is tough hunting and rough living. It was difficult for me as well, but walking in a prime mountain elk area with not a single boot track in the dusty pack route helped me relax and focus. Backcountry hunting opened him an entirely new universe of opportunities.

Being "in deep" seemed to me to be a tremendous equaliser. It was one of the few places I knew where money and status didn't help with the hunt. Back home, I was a warehouse worker, but putting good bulls and bucks on the ground in the mountains made me feel like I could accomplish amazing things. The outdoors had a tremendous impact on me as a young man looking for a path in life. However, learning the ropes in the bush and attempting to shoot an elk with my bow gave me that old familiar feeling of doing the

impossible. Back there, the elk hunting was fierce...Wild country, highly strung elk, on edge from living in an exceedingly harsh environment while attempting to avoid the natural born killers of the mountains, cougars, were extremely difficult to come in bow range of. As a solitary hunter, the frightening length of Oregon's greatest wilderness area rattled my confidence. I sometimes worried if I had what it takes to get things done "in depth."
I did.
And releasing this altered my life forever.
Life is a trial. Sometimes you discover you're not passing a class and need to adjust your study habits. Similar to what happened when our first child was born. I wondered what I was doing with my life once I held Tanner in my arms. I knew I had to improve. Suddenly, it wasn't only myself who was failing. Now I had a life that depended on me, and it came with a legacy.
What was I going to leave behind?
I honestly didn't know. I didn't have a clear path or response. I didn't have a degree, and I didn't have anyone by my side offering good guidance or even solid advice for a new father. I didn't know what I was doing, so I had to learn by trial and error. Like everything else in my life. There was never a grand strategy, or, to be honest, any plan at all. It's just been a matter of doing what I can each day.
When I understood that things needed to change, I reasoned, "Well, all I really know how to do is work." So I decided to put in as many hours as I could. That was all I had to offer: my hard work. I started putting in long hours and noticed that guys would listen to me. I could persuade them to do things that other guys couldn't. I'm not sure why, but when some males talk, people dismiss them, and when other guys talk, people listen and think to themselves, "Okay, that makes sense." I knew I had some leadership characteristics, and that, combined with my willingness to work my buttocks off, led to more opportunities. That's how my career began.
When a hunting article I wrote was published decades ago, the publisher included a profile that wrongly stated that I was a warehouse supervisor rather than the lead. Tim, a nasty coworker, brought it up, laughing loudly and telling everyone, "Cam thinks he's a supervisor." He's just a starting point." Finally, on the same day I was formally promoted to supervisor, I took a job on the construction

team at my current workplace. Except that I'm now the superintendent. Tim, are you still laughing?

When I was offered a job on the construction team for the Springfield Utility Board (SUB) in 1996, it was for less money than I was making as a supervisor at the Coast-to-Coast distribution centre, but I took it nevertheless. Everyone knows that working for the city, state, or municipality is a nice and stable employment, therefore despite the sacrifice, my younger self made a decent decision. Actually, that was a wise decision. Since then, I've been employed with the Springfield Utility Board.

I used to believe that if I got a nice job like this, I'd have everything I ever wanted. Working for a fantastic firm and getting a nice job with good perks. I felt like the luckiest guy in the world after I started working. I was now going to look after my family. We acquired our first house for $64,000, which I later fixed up and sold for $91,000. We used that equity to buy a somewhat larger house in a more humble neighbourhood. Everything was going in the correct direction.

However, because of the new work, I didn't have any vacation time yet, so I couldn't go hunting in the wilderness for 10 days like I had in previous seasons. I had to become a "weekend warrior" instead. It was simply another sacrifice I was willing to make.

Some of those weekends are still vivid in my mind. I would mountain bike into the logging region where I grew up hunting, parked at the mainline gate and biking for hours before sunrise to be miles in before the sun came up. I wanted to be further in than everybody else so that I could hunt animals without being disturbed.

I didn't need to go to Eagle Cap to get as far away from other hunters as feasible.

I glassed up a herd of elk miles distant from my high vantage point one fateful morning as a late summer rain poured gently. I was on the 9,000 line, and the elk were back off the 5,000, so I'd rode right by them. It also meant that other hunters who didn't venture as far as I did could be closer to them. I went on my bike, blasted down, reached the mainline, and hammered my pedals like a bowhunting Lance Armstrong, chewing up the miles. When I reached the 5,000 mark, it was all uphill to the road that would take me closest to the herd. My quadriceps were on fire when I sat in the seat and pushed hard on the pedals. Because there isn't enough weight on the back tire, it will dig up the rocks if you stand up and peddle. So you sit and work. I'd been scouting up there all summer, so my legs were in great shape, allowing me to get to the elk quickly.

I didn't have good optics, so I couldn't determine how big the bull was from a distance, but I knew he was at the head of the herd. I moved closer to where I'd last seen them, an arrow in my hand. My strategy was flawless. I stalked closer while the animal remained bedded. As I approached full draw, the bull was facing me. I expected him to stand because he looked at me as soon as I settled in for the shot. Instead, he remained in his bed. I had a lot of confidence in my shot at forty-three yards, built up over time and repetition, so I locked my forty-yard pin high, just over the space where his shoulder and sternum connect, and released. The arrow landed neatly on the nock. As blood flowed from the wound in his chest, the large-bodied bull stood. Because it was a heart shot, he didn't get far before collapsing in the thick reprod.

A wonderful weekend warrior shot.

I was still called to the outdoors, so I'd blast across the state whenever I could. Weekend scouting or hunting trips might look like this: I left work about 4:00 p.m. on Friday afternoon, travelling north via Portland till I arrived at my Eagle Cap trailhead at 1:00 a.m. I'd pick up my bag and set out, hoping to make it back to the house by first light. I couldn't fall asleep. I'd return to the wilderness before first light on Saturday and be able to hunt or scout until Sunday. Then I'd hike out and drive home on Sunday night, returning to work on Monday.

It was worth two nights of no sleep for two days of reconnaissance, or hunting if it was season. These adventures gave me the courage to embark on extended solo hunts. I was putting myself through tests and passing them all.

As time passed, and elk hunting became such a passion—an obsession—that I eventually used up all of my vacation time, my supervisor told me I couldn't miss another day of work. I wasn't on the crew anymore; I was now the buyer, which gave me more leeway because other crew members weren't reliant on me. As a buyer, if I was absent, the work would simply pile up until I returned. Nonetheless, I had exhausted my vacation time. I informed them that it appeared we would have to make a choice. They might not have believed I was worth the ultimatum if I hadn't gained their trust and confidence and proven my worth. Instead, they allowed me to go hunting, and I made up the time when I returned.

Would most individuals risk their jobs—steady, good jobs—to pursue a hobby? Most likely not. The majority of people are wiser and more practical than I am.

I'm relieved I did.

Don't make excuses.
Give it your all.
Show up when you're supposed to show up.
Speak your mind.
Own up to your mistakes.
Think with perspective.
This is how you live a life worth remembering. That's what I was starting to do.

The world, including I, will never forget August 31, 1997. Of course, I'm not like everyone else.
This was my eighth season as a bowhunter, and my world centred on survival, eating, drinking, shelter, and, of course, killing a bull on that fateful day.
That was the end of it.
Nothing else was important.
I was returning from a hunt with exciting news to share with my wife. I contacted her when I got in my Toyota and finally got cell service on the freeway.
"Hello, Trace. "I slain a six-by-six bull."
It was the most impressive bull I'd ever slaughtered. I wasn't expecting her response.
"Princess Diana died."
"What?"
"Princess Di passed away. She was involved in an automobile accident in Paris."
"Who cares?" I exclaimed.
I know it seems callous, but look... Nothing else matters when you're back in the bush and kill a six-by-six bull. Princess Diana was stunning and had a huge heart. She was an icon to the highest degree, and her death was a tragedy. Her funeral was seen by about 2.5 billion people. I see what you're saying.
But for a twenty-nine-year-old me in late August of 1997, the only thing on my mind was arrowing a decent wilderness bull. And this six-by-six was my best at the time.
Please forgive my selfishness, Princess Di.
We kept in touch via phone while Roy and his family were in Alaska, providing each other updates on our hunting adventures. I'd tell him about my kills and tell him some anecdotes, and he'd tell me

about his hunting and guiding adventures. We'd occasionally phone each other simply to BS. We attempted to get together at least once a year to pull off something spectacular. My first two trips to Alaska were in 1997 to hunt Sitka blacktail deer on Kodiak Island and in 1999 to hunt black bear on Prince of Wales Island. Over the years, I've probably hunted in Alaska thirty times. We had incredible trips together.

I still remember going up the Dalton Highway into the Prudhoe Bay Oil Field in northern Alaska for fifteen hours. That's basically where the roadway ends up at the top of the world. It's a long way up there. You assumed that if you went to a specific vantage point, you could see the curvature of the earth. There was nothing except wonderful, wild hunting up there, which was more than enough for us. We did a forty-mile float trip on our own, killing caribou with our bows, getting chased by a grizzly, and living on the edge for a week.

Our path has been fuelled by enormous ideas since the beginning. Roy and I used to be fierce competitors, even with each other. When I was twenty and Roy was twenty-two, we used to knock each other out of the way as we struggled for a shot at a big bull elk. We debated about tactics, gear, and everything else like brothers would. We were successful as hunters on a limited scale that suited the little town and world we called home. We also know that success often creates jealousy, so some people sought to undermine our bowhunting exploits in the early years. All of this did was drive us to strive harder, making us not just stronger as individuals, but also as bowhunting brothers with an unbreakable relationship.

I believe this unbreakable bond was formed because, for many years early on, our mindset in bowhunting was, "It's us against everyone else." The truth is that it wasn't. While some may have talked smack, a smack-talker can only go so far. When we were in a huge, isolated area, we knew there wouldn't be any head-to-head competition in bowhunting. It's just man vs beast, country versus himself. In any case, the us-versus-them mental games kept us concentrated and always striving to outwork the imaginary bow hunting animals with whom we competed in our heads.

Roy was the only other guy I'd ever hunted with who had no boundaries. He, like me, wanted to go further. If he wanted to push harder, past where most people would give up, so did I. The agony we had to undergo was meaningless. We endured a great deal of bodily and mental anguish while surviving difficult hunts in those early years.

This is most likely why I never found anyone else to go hunting with. Roy and I both had families to support, and we both worked. But everyday life was quite monotonous for us, which we frequently joked about whenever we were together. We knew everyone was talented in some way. Some guys excelled as insurance salespeople, builders, teachers, and doctors; we excelled in completing difficult bowhunts.

"Cam, it's what we do."

Roy often stated this to us when we defied the odds and put ourselves to the test. This was why we lived. Our daily lives couldn't have been more dissimilar than what stirred our souls.

For many years, bowhunting was a challenge that defined Roy and me and gave us an identity. I know we were both probably too preoccupied with hunting early on. Roy did a better job of prioritising than I did over the years, even though the mountains still beckoned to him fiercely. Like everything else in my life, I've gotten better at it over time.

I've been with the same company for over twenty-five years.

I've never missed work due to illness.

I've never missed a day that wasn't scheduled for me to be away.

People always wonder why I don't just quit my day job because I make more money from my side hustle of bowhunting. Because my work ethic is the only reason I excel, and my employment at the utility company has played a significant role in building that work ethic, I feel compelled to remain and continue working there. I adore the men who work for me. I believe in them and wish them well. Maybe I'm just a good person?

Also, I don't give up easily. I'm not going to begin now.

Getting that job meant everything to me, so it would be difficult for me to say, "Hey, I'm putting in my two weeks' notice so I can be a full-time bowhunter." I'm not sure if I'll ever be able to achieve it. I still go on hunts and make appearances during my vacation time. Balancing it all simply means that I have to work harder every day. I enjoy working where I work, so there doesn't seem to be much of a choice. This is my job.

I'm a labourer.

The truth is that I've always worked extremely hard since I've never felt like I had a lot of natural aptitude or talents. Not having regular work would feel weird to me. I feel like such a life is saved for a star, and I don't think I'm one, so I grind it out. I work hard at training and I work hard at work.

My one advantage is that I never take a day off. I can't just say, "You know, I'm not going to run today." "I've made enough sacrifices."

No.

That is something that everyone does. Everyone has an explanation. Everyone has an explanation. You can always find an excuse not to take on a challenge. So I've learnt to disregard the excuse. It's never true. That's my approach, and that's my competitive advantage. It's how I've developed endurance and resilience. My schedule contains no rest days. That is why I am successful.

It's not a lack of talent. No such luck. There is no expertise.

It's called discipline. Endurance. Work ethics are important.

I've heard the same explanations for the last thirty years or more.

"Yeah, I'd do badass bowhunts as well." But I have children."

So do I.

"I wish I could train like you and shoot my bow all the time, but I have a full-time job."

Yes, I agree.

I've always been a hard worker, but that's only the beginning. You cannot simply have a work ethic; you must earn it. Discipline and perfection are not something that can be imagined and then achieved. Make a resolution to do something every day for a year. Find something that will help you improve yourself and do it every day for a year, whether it's running a mile, reading a chapter, writing a paragraph, eating breakfast, or drinking a gallon of water.

That is how you develop a work ethic.

CHAPTER 6:
OBSESSED OR AVERAGE

Either improve and evolve, or throw in the towel. These are the two options we face on a daily basis. Growth might be as easy as suddenly deciding to go run outside in the rain, or it can be a deep-seated urge you've had since childhood.

Hunting isn't the only thing I've been interested in since I was a child. A delicious elk steak can motivate anyone, but the written word has always been a source of inspiration for me. I grew up obsessed with superb writing, especially about hunting, but the subject didn't really matter. I was attracted by words that could paint a picture. I was never very good at writing, but I wanted to be and worked very hard to improve. As I previously stated, Hunting with the Bow and Arrow by Saxton Pope, with a special introduction by Fred Bear, is one of my favourite books. My father purchased the title during one of his frequent Salvation Army bargain hunts. I lost myself in that book, and its images are seared into my memory.

I used to buy and read every hunting magazine on the shelf when I was a youngster. I've always enjoyed the feel, scent, images, and, of course, the words that can be found in good hunting magazines. Magazine articles have been framed and cutout magazine articles have been used to fill albums. I have stacks of hunting publications that drive my wife insane that I would never dream of getting rid of. They are an ingrained part of my bowhunting past, if you will. As a kid, I'd ride through the woods of western Oregon, recalling stories from my favourite hunting writers. This was a special time in my life. All of the magazines featured excellent writers, but the stories in Bowhunter magazine seemed to speak to me the most. I was young, but it was the biggest, greatest, and most legitimate magazine in the world to me.

In the same way that today's youth idolise professional athletes, I looked up to my "hunting idols." To me, they were larger than life. Back in the late 1980s, in my dark living room, the TV flickered and emanated noises of screaming bull elk while I watched my grainy Elk Fever VHS tape so many times that I could quote nearly every phrase Dwight Schuh and Larry D. Jones spoke. I remember the "pinecones-in-the-boot" trick, as well as all of the fantastic bowhunting activity, clearly. I got Dwight's green wool gloves and fletched my arrows with red and white vanes just like him. I wore camo face paint with white and grey hues blended in, exactly like Larry, and I always put my middle initial in the byline, just like Larry D. Jones.

M. R. James, the magazine's editor at the time, was also an influential figure for a kid who bled bowhunting. During those early years, I even put a bandana over my neck when bowhunting, as I'd seen M. R. do in numerous magazine articles.

My obsession was not restricted to my Bowhunter magazine idols. I didn't smile at my first few kills since I was attempting to resemble a prominent name in bowhunting at the time, Myles Keller. Chuck Adams, of course, was the bowhunting king, and I took great delight in the fact that he, too, grew up hunting blacktails.

The late Billy Cruise, founder of Oregon Bow and an elk-hunting legend in Oregon's Eagle Cap Wilderness, was a godlike figure to me in terms of hometown heroes. Billy's incredible stories of backcountry success in the same area and drainages where I bowhunted for large bulls pushed me to be harder and endure more than I would have otherwise. Because of him, I began shooting an Oregon Bow, and I will never forget being featured in my first magazine advertising for Oregon Bow. My life was governed by my enthusiasm for bowhunting back then. Nothing has changed.

My first hunting essay was published in 1990, not long after my first bow season in 1989. After blowing my opportunity at a monster, I penned a narrative called "Bulls, Bugles, and Botches" about the spike bull I killed my first season as a bowhunter.

I had everything sorted out in my own little world. So I reasoned.

Everyone requires feedback. But obtaining honest feedback isn't often easy. "Yeah, I think it sounds really good," most people would respond after reading my work. Excellent work." That drove me insane since I knew it wasn't fantastic but couldn't pinpoint why.

Carl Allen didn't mind telling me the truth. I met Trace at the same warehouse where I worked with him. Carl was an interesting character in a sea of them at work. While working and bickering, he and his wife would yell at each other over the warehouse intercom and throw trash cans at each other. He was a hippie and a little crazy. He wasn't a hunter, but he was well-read and knowledgeable. I decided to have him read an essay I wrote for Western Bowhunter one day. I understood writers' desires and required feedback. You put your heart out there, thus you must finally ask someone, "What do you think about my heart?"

So I approached Carl and requested him to read my piece. He understood outstanding writing even though he couldn't relate to travelling into the forest to hunt for elk.

He read it and didn't say much more than "Good job." Instead, he inquired, "How is it like stalking the animal?" What sounds are you hearing? What does it sound like when you take steps? Could you just put me there? "Could you tell me what it was like to be you right now, how you felt?"

Carl's advice was quite beneficial.

"I want to be there with you on the hunt," that's what he said. "I want you to paint that picture with your words and put me there."

"OK," I answered simply. Then it hit me: Oh my God, he's correct. I need to bring folks along with me on these hunts. I need to show them what it's like to stalk a buck with an arrow in my hand, the wind gently blowing on my face, ensuring me that my scent won't reach the deer before my arrow does.

Carl's feedback provided me with insight and encouragement to delve further into my writing. I was used to delving further into the woods when hunting, so I felt quite at home pushing deeper into my writing. Trying to improve my attention to detail. Trying to paint a more vivid picture using the words on the page.

The first step toward improvement after getting constructive criticism is to act on it.

I was all in.

I made my name as a writer by writing many how-to articles and editing a hunting magazine, Eastmans' Bowhunting Journal, but all I really wanted to do was write hunting adventure pieces because that's what I enjoyed reading as a reader. The magazine industry demanded technical articles and how-tos, but I was truly invested only when I was writing of large enterprises, thus before I worked for Eastmans', I wanted to go big.

A gifted writer is required to write big adventures. And, like I'd done for most of my life, I'd put the cart before the horse.

To me, the ideal way to start my writing career was to get an essay published in Bowhunter, the world's top bowhunting magazine. So, following a successful season in 1994, which included arrowing two

Pope & Young blacktail bucks, I put together a manuscript package and mailed it to M. R. James. I was ecstatic about my first possible Bowhunter feature.

After sending my essay to M. R., I began calling home every day from work, asking Tracey whether anything from the magazine had arrived in the mail. Every day, I received the same response from my wife: "Nope, Cam, nothing today."

Then, a few months later, it finally happened. I remember it like it was yesterday. I dialled home after going upstairs to the warehouse lunchroom for my midday break. Tracey answered the phone and stated, "You got something from Bowhunter."

I told her to open it with butterflies in my stomach. I heard ripping and tearing, the phone ringing, and Tracey said I received a letter and some other items from someone named M. R. James. She began reading the note.

"To Cameron, Thank you for submitting your 'Bonus Bucks' manuscript. Congratulations on obtaining two excellent bowhunting trophies. I'm returning your article and photographs, as well as an opportunity to rework and resubmit it."

A full page of excellent advice followed, and the message closed with these words: "Rewrite your article and try us again." You have the makings of a fantastic deer essay, but getting it ready for publication in Bowhunter will take some work. Good luck, and please let me know if you require any specific editorial assistance. Regards, M. R. James."

I knew where the letter was going after Tracey read me the second sentence. I was devastated. I'd wanted to be an outdoors writer ever since I killed my first deer at the age of fifteen and wrote a tale about it in English class. My dreams had been destroyed.

Rewrite and resubmit?

I had no desire to rewrite anything. I'd worked very hard on that article, poured my heart and soul into it, and was confident that every single word was perfect.

With a "I'll show you" attitude, I viciously forwarded the essay, as is, to a local hunting magazine, which published it and issued me a nice large check for $25.

In reality, that was around $25 more than the article was worth. My article was simply a hunting story about a guy who got lucky and

shot two big bucks. It didn't educate the reader anything, nor did it provide any compelling insights or lessons. While I was upset and frustrated at the time, M. R. was correct. My article did not meet Bowhunter's requirements. However, this bitter disappointment was crucial for my growth as a writer. I took a chance and was forced to choose between improving and growing or giving up.
I decided to keep hammering.

What are you willing to give up?
You must make sacrifices in order to achieve anything in life. Not simply the conventional ones we consider, such as money and time. You may have to give up your emotional energy or others' confidence and believe in you. Everything for the sake of a dream.
One person's dreams are never the same as another's. T. E. Lawrence, popularly known as Lawrence of Arabia, was a British academic, writer, and soldier who once stated of dreams, "All men dream: but not equally." Those who dream at night in the dusty caverns of their thoughts awake in the morning to realise that it was vanity; but daydreamers are dangerous persons, for they may act their dreams with wide eyes, to make it possible."
Sacrifice is the only way to make dreams come true.
I was writing for a magazine called Western Bowhunter for free back in the mid-1990s, when no one knew who I was. All I wanted to be was a writer, but I wasn't really one. When Doug Walker, the editor of Western Bowhunter, asked if I wanted to go on a writer's hunt he was organising, I agreed despite the fact that it would cost me around $3,000. I had no business travelling to bow hunt at the time, but I didn't care. My ambitions exceeded my ability and, most emphatically, my financial resources.
We were impoverished at the time. We had just born our first child (Tanner), so Trace was on maternity leave for six weeks while I was earning roughly twelve dollars an hour. We were on the WIC nutritional food program for six weeks until Trace returned to work. Spending $300 would have been out of the question, but $3,000? That would have been absurd, and it was.
One part of me realised this was a chance, but another part warned me I'd never get that money back. Even if I were paid $25 per piece, as I was when I wrote for Oregon Hunter, how many articles would I have to write to earn back $3,000? How many articles are there in a

year? I was only hunting in Oregon at the time, so how many articles could I possibly write? I didn't have to be a genius to see that the maths on this was off.

After my in-laws offered me $200 toward the search, I decided to charge the remainder to my credit card and treat it as a business venture. I could use this hunt to establish a brand and begin selling hunting articles to cover my monthly credit card payment. The hunt would only take around five years to pay off.

Oh, to be young and filled with unrealistic expectations.

Yeah, in the near run, I recognize that was a bad decision. To pay off that quest, I worked as many hours as I could at the warehouse where I was employed, sometimes up to sixteen hours a day. Until I wrote my books, I probably spent a hundred times more money than I ever made as a hunting writer.

I had vivid memories of the hunt. It occurred on the YO Ranch in Texas, which was so large that the killings counted as free range, which isn't typically the case in Texas. I could have killed two whitetail deer for the price I paid. The first was a little eight-point deer, and the second was a management seven-point buck. But I went on vacation and never looked back.

This is the kind of mindset you must have.

Are you willing to put yourself out there?

Are you willing and able to be so stupid?

I knew it wasn't a good idea, but I did it all the time and convinced myself that it would pay off someday. I didn't worry about whether I'd get my money back or how quickly I'd get it. I didn't wonder where this was going to lead me.

My mindset was to leave. To have faith. To take a risk. To be daring and try again and again.

Obsession is isolating. Bowhunting has been my preoccupation for the past thirty-three Septembers.

Some people will look at me and say nonsense. They have no idea of the sacrifices and challenges I've endured over the years. I've discovered that those who talk the most will not sacrifice what I have, and those who will will not talk shit. Because they understand.

All I know is that you don't need anyone else to believe in your vision. You can be anyone you want to be if you have tunnel vision.

There was never a major scheme. I decided one day that I wanted to write a novel that was kickass. Full-colour hardcover. Nobody had ever written a book about blacktail bowhunting, so that's what I set out to accomplish. That was the extent of it. What would the price be? I calculated how much it would cost to print them and how much I should charge for each copy.

It found out that printing 5,000 copies would cost $50,000. That was around $50,000 more than I had. I chose to publish the book regardless. I had to borrow money from everyone in my family. As the largest investment, my grandmother Ruby ended up giving me roughly $15,000.

Was it a bad idea to go ahead with a full-colour hardback book? Yeah. But I paid back everyone, including my grandmother. She was so surprised that I gave her the money. She never had anyone in her family repay her because, unfortunately, that's how families work. "Yeah, I'll pay you back," it's always like, but then things happen. But that's exactly what I did: I paid off my debt. I've always been someone who does what I say. The only thing I ask is that others keep their end of the contract, whatever it may be.

I took my time, but I eventually sold all 5,000 copies of Bowhunting Trophy Blacktail. We had a lot of bookcases in the house for a long time, and I even had to relocate them once to a different house. I didn't give it much thought before publishing it, which is why it wasn't very profitable. I didn't make a business plan or anything like that. I simply believed and determined that I needed to write and self-publish that book.

I had a bigger brand and a publisher by the time I wrote my second book, Backcountry Bowhunting, in 2005, and that particular title blew out. It is now in its eighth printing, with 90,000 copies sold. Those two volumes were two more major risks I took on myself, not only in the realm of bowhunting but also in my other passion, writing.

It took me twenty years to eventually gain a few Bowhunter pages. I finally had a featured piece named "Bleed" in the September 2009 issue, complete with the byline "Cameron R. Hanes" published in the table of contents, after twenty long, hard years. During those two decades, I wrote hundreds of magazine articles, penned two books, served as editor of a bowhunting magazine for ten years, refined my bowhunting and writing talents, and worked tirelessly to raise three children as best I could—all with Tracey's unflinching support. And now, as our odyssey comes to a close, I've been given the opportunity to write a regular column for my favourite bowhunting publication.

Bowhunting has shaped my personality. When I think about bowhunting, I imagine myself trudging up faint pack routes in the bush to lonely, craggy mountains. Nothing about the backcountry hunts I enjoy is simple. Bowhunting, in my opinion, will make you want to cry at times, will have you dripping with sweat most of the time, and will almost certainly require you to bleed a little for success.

I was browsing through some stuff in my office at work not long ago when I came across a flyer Eastmans' created to promote my book, Backcountry Bowhunting. As I read the personal endorsements my book received from celebrities, a few thoughts came to me.

To begin, I'm sure there are people on social media who have never heard of Chuck Adams, Mike Eastman, Randy Ulmer, or Dwight Schuh. They are all hunting legends who inspired me as I learned the ropes as a bowhunter and writer. They set the path for many in the hunting industry and had a big influence on me. I'd be lurking in the mountains, arrow at the ready, eyes searching, thinking about Chuck Adams and those Sitka blacktails he'd hunt on Kodiak Island in the late summer, or that famous photo of him with his enormous bow-killed brown bear. I'd remember his hat, his smile, and those seemingly enormous aluminium arrows by today's standards. I wished I could be Chuck Adams. I attempted to imitate his tunnel vision focus. I didn't have deep pockets, and I was new to bowhunting, but I made up for it with determination. I discovered more than thirty years ago that with tremendous effort, I could achieve above-average hunting outcomes.

Hunters such as Chuck Adams and Randy Ulmer just set the standard for outstanding bowhunting. For years, I read their essays and looked at their images, pining for the experiences they'd had. I continue to do so. When Mike Eastman offered me a job at Eastmans', he believed in me when few others did and gave me a career-changing chance. The late Dwight Schuh demonstrated the "power of the pen" to me. For decades, his writing has inspired me. And, as talented as he was as a writer, he was an even better man. I felt privileged to have known him.

The second thing that occurred to me was how the warm and kind comments they had written about me and my book felt strange when this flyer appeared. They continue to do so even today. One thing I've found is that jealousy and envy can pervade and poison the outdoor sector. Our egos have us tearing one other down instead of building each other up and becoming a stronger community of cohesive, passionate, and focused hunters with a shared interest. We can't really afford to split ourselves because of our small size. We rely on one another. What these four pioneers said about me as I struggled to make my way speaks a lot about me. They didn't have to build me up. To me, this speaks a lot about the men they are, and it goes a long way toward explaining why they've become hunting, writing, and outdoor icons.

I'm still thankful, proud, and grateful that those icons paved the road for me.

On December 10, 1962, John Steinbeck accepted the Nobel Prize in Literature for "his realistic and imaginative writings, which combine sympathetic humour and keen social perception." His introductory words made it plain that winning this accolade made him feel a little like an impostor.

"In my heart there may be doubt that I deserve the Nobel award over other men of letters whom I hold in respect and reverence—but there is no question of my pleasure and pride in having it for myself,"

I've felt like an impostor myself, which has pushed me to work harder at what I do. Running, training, hunting, and even writing are all options.

"The writer is delegated to declare and celebrate man's proven capacity for greatness of heart and spirit—for gallantry in defeat, for courage, compassion, and love," says Steinbeck. These are the bright rally flags of hope and emulation in the never-ending struggle against weakness and despair. A writer who does not believe in man's perfectibility, in my opinion, has neither dedication nor membership in literature."

Steinbeck isn't talking about being "perfect," but rather the road and perseverance to achieving perfection. This brings back memories of my own trip.

My ambition for bowhunting perfection.

My hopes for publishing stories based on those adventures.

Man's perfectibility reminds me of my first 100-mile endurance race in 2009. I consider the enthusiasm I see in others and the success I see in others.

What is your ambition? My goal is to become the "perfect" bowhunter. I want to be successful on every hunt and release a perfect arrow that results in the animals I pursue dying quickly and mercifully. I believe bowhunting is unlikely to be mastered, yet that is my desire.

That was the start of my running and training journey. Greatness can only be attained via hard work. To strive for perfection, you must invest everything you have in your aspirations.

It was time to become fully obsessed.

CHAPTER 7:
RAMP IT UP

You must first walk before you can run.

Hunting and running used to go together like oil and water. I ran to get in shape and knew it helped my hunting, but no one ever mentioned hunting exercise. There was no massive athletic performance apparel company like Under Armour manufacturing the highest-quality gear for the active hunter and projecting to everyone who would listen, "Athletes hunt."

I began running just for the sake of the exam, to challenge myself.

I had never run more than a 10K before the year 2000. Then I entered a 7.3-mile race in Salem, Oregon, and the guys thought I was insane for running that far merely to get in condition to hunt the blacktail forests near my house. Then I ran a half-marathon, and in 2003, I finished third overall in my first marathon.

This was around the time I realised my physical condition may have a significant impact in the hunting woods. This was an area where I could improve. During a hunt, I may hike twenty miles or more in a single day, so stamina is essential. In general, the better shape I was in, the easier it was to succeed. And I've yet to find a limit to this method. But I'm trying.

I've raced in ultramarathons since that first marathon, and when I'm in peak fitness, just before bow season, I run at least twenty kilometres a day. I've increased my efforts in order to build both physical and mental strength, and it's paid off with many years of constant achievement. For many of the same reasons that I enjoy bowhunting, I enjoy endurance running. Both disciplines will test even the toughest of human beings at times. And, in both cases, justice is always served in the long run, as those who work the hardest and make the most sacrifices gain the benefits.

But believe me when I say this wasn't easy. And believe me when I say that if I can do it, so can you.

You must put forth persistent effort no matter where you begin.

I wasn't born with the ability to run. I used to have trouble running three miles. I understand how you feel.

You have to get off the sofa and start moving before you can grind your way to the top of a mountain.

So, where do you begin?

As I've said before, I don't give advice; I simply express what I know. And I am aware that what I do is not for everyone. Maybe it's not for everyone else. To see where your trip can take you, you must first begin. My entire point is that it doesn't matter what you do—whether you run or hike—as long as you're walking and moving.

It's fine if you've never run before. Get out there and walk about your neighbourhood. Go somewhere and do something just to burn some calories and rev up your metabolism. Walk whenever you can, even if it's only for a half hour; you'll feel better for it. You'll be shocked at how far you've gone in just a couple of weeks of going for frequent walks. Then begin incorporating some running. Walk for five minutes, run for five minutes, walk for another five minutes, and then run for five minutes. You'll gradually begin to run more. Walk for five minutes and then run for ten, then walk for five minutes and then run for ten.

You'll soon find yourself running the entire time. Then you can place some hills there, but go slowly. Few people can run up a hill. It's fantastic if you can, but you don't start out going uphill.

Nothing beats running in the mountains, but I've worked up to it. I see a lot of guys who start running and push themselves too hard right away, resulting in shin splints. They are then powerless to act. You're using muscles that you don't regularly use in ordinary life, and you need to build them up before going wild. You have to ease into running, and you have to put in the time and effort.

My running progressed with time. When I started running fifty miles per week, I was quickly able to run a half-marathon in under 1:20. I still didn't feel I was talented or naturally gifted as a runner after finishing third in my first marathon. I just knew I worked extremely hard and that I could work even more.

I am not endowed with extraordinary talent. Time is my secret. And I've been working hard for years to get where I am now.

I quickly figured it out during my first year in the woods with a bow in hand. I remember thinking it would be impossible to reach within bow range of a bull elk and knock him down with one of my arrows. Nobody informed me I'd feel completely safe in the elk-infested forests with my stick and thread. But I persisted, and each day I learnt something new.

Day after day, day after day, day after day.

I was finally getting it with each passing day, and the work paid off when I arrowed a spike bull elk after eighteen days of bowhunting. What is the key to that success? Time. I took that young bull after nearly three weeks of elk hunting, every day putting forth a valiant effort. But nothing happens overnight in something as difficult as bowhunting.

In terms of skill, I am probably 10 times the bowhunter I was back then. The main reason for this is because I'm never satisfied. I am constantly striving to improve. Get in fitness, become a better shot, and a more knowledgeable hunter.

This will take time.

In this day and age of quick satisfaction, you cannot expect results overnight.

Of course, like most people, I expected those immediate effects right away. That was part of being young and stupid.

I still had a lot to learn. And, as Michelangelo famously said, "I am still learning."

I'm always looking for a harder and tougher task to put myself through. After discovering that I could run marathons, I began researching ultramarathons. I ran the McDonald Forest 50K (32 miles) in 2005. People in my small circle thought I was insane yet again, and as I ran, I had a few ideas that they were correct. It was the most difficult thing I had ever done, and I promised never to do it again. Of course, I ran in the event on a regular basis in the years that followed.

I opted to participate in the Bighorn Trail Run in 2007. In the three weeks leading up to the event, I posted a daily "Day in the Life" on my blog, detailing how I prepared for the big race. Here's an excerpt from a post written ten days before the race:

4:00 a.m.: I'm up, I couldn't sleep. Shower, emails, eat cereal soaked in water, read the paper, check a couple forums, and coffee on the way to work. On the way out the door my wife had to remind me today is our 15th anniversary. Man, talk about having a pit in my stomach. Not saying I forgot, but it has been a very busy time.
Supplements: Multivitamin, calcium, magnesium, vitamin D, Vitamineral Green drink mix, and fish oil capsule.
6:00 a.m.: Work, fire off 30 pull-ups right out of the gate. Feeling not-so-fresh yet this morning. It was a short night of sleep.
10:00 a.m.: Coffee and a whole wheat roll.

12:00 p.m.: Eat two chicken and black bean burritos, watermelon, two pieces of wheat bread with no butter that Tracey delivered, like every day. She is the best. Drink water.

4:00 p.m.: Get home and chill out with the kids. Eat a little steak and whole wheat noodles. Light meal. Take off on a run with a Spott Hogg SDP sight with wrap that I will drop off at the Bow Rack during my run. Wayne set up my Vectrix and Vectrix XL with the red, white, and blue custom string. I did shoot a couple times before heading home. MONEY through paper in two shots with the Vectrix. God, that is a sweet feeling. Run home (this is an easy six-mile run all together), shoot the Vulcan 24 times before running out the door, taking a hand-off from Trace of a bowlful of noodles and steak as I go. I shovel it down on the way to the first of Tanner's two summer league basketball games.

6:30 to 9:30 p.m.: Watch B-ball (Tanner played well) and work on the computer. Emails. Lots of emails to get back to. This daily blog has really stirred interest. I love it. I can talk about bowhunting and conditioning as it relates to bowhunting all day and night. It sure seems like more guys are wanting to do all they can to prepare themselves for the rigours of the backcountry these days. This will result in bowhunting effectiveness, and more success means the tradition of bowhunting grows. That is my number one objective.

One thing I'd like to share in this space: Do not think you need to go on 10-, 20-, or 80-mile runs to be a successful bowhunter. I do think the more you can do, the better off you'll be. Especially in the mountains. That being said, many many guys kill animals with their bows and don't run a step before the season. For that matter, there are guys who arrow animals every year who dusted off their bows a week before the opener. The problem in keeping up that routine is that those guys might not kill anything for five or ten more years. For the average guy, if you don't prepare your body and you don't practise, if you kill anything with a bow, it will be in large part because of LUCK.

Bowhunting is all about preparation, and my goal is to hopefully inspire guys to ramp up what they are currently doing to prepare. If you run three miles once a week, maybe this blog will motivate you to run three times a week? If you shoot your bow twice a week, maybe after reading this you will shoot four times a week? Look, I am not saying what I do, you should too. I am saying whatever we have called the "norm," we can do more. That is me, you, everyone. Do this and bowhunting wins. Again, success and sharing positive experiences grows bowhunting. Pump the passion for the sport. Are you doing all you can?

As is customary, I explained what I was doing rather than advising people what they should do. The most obvious thing anyone could see was that if I established a goal, I was 100% committed, physically and psychologically, to being the best I could be. My goal was to train for the insanely difficult 32.4-mile Bighorn Trail Run in Wyoming's Bighorn Mountains and finish with my greatest ultramarathon finish ever. (An ultramarathon is a race that goes longer than 26 miles.) My previous best finish was sixth in the 2006 Siskiyou Out & Back Trail Run (called the SOB) in Ashland, Oregon. This purpose for running the Bighorn (where I finished second, if memory serves) was to maybe demonstrate to folks who have a negative perception of hunters that we are a passionate group of people. All of my conditioning efforts were directed solely toward bowhunting.

We all experience and accept the call to adventure if we are all heroes and heroines on quests and travels, as Joseph Campbell wrote about in The Hero with a Thousand Faces. When I decided to pursue bowhunting as a hobby and to become the best hunter I could be, I accepted mine. We eventually reach a point of no return and must conquer any hurdles that stand in our way of progress. These can be deep-seated concerns or discouraging justifications that keep us from moving forward. This is referred to by Campbell as "crossing the first threshold."

When you're getting off the couch and out the door, it's natural not to want to travel more into the unknown, knowing that whatever follows next will be more tough. I did this when I first started bowhunting, and I continued to do so when I went backcountry bowhunting on my own after Roy moved. I was now pushing myself even more by jogging greater distances.
Ultramarathons? What on earth was I thinking?
I stood at the entrance, which, as Campbell put it, leads to "darkness, the unknown, and danger." Of course, anything like that piqued my interest. Except for Roy Roth, no one else may comprehend this.
No peak is too high, no challenge too tremendous, and danger is non-existent.
Roy, while not a runner like me, certainly understood the attitude that drove me to compete in the Bighorn Trail Run.
I was prepared.

I started the race with a plan. My plan was to go out aggressively and "break" the other racers by hammering out the first fourteen miles, which featured some difficult ascents (up to 9,000 feet) and harsh descents on game trails. This part had it all: jumping over logs, sliding through mud, and sloshing through snow. I was knocked out twice. Tripping down the steep slopes and flying like Superman, but not really. With my arms outstretched, I was skidding down the hill over pebbles, sticks, and muck. That last bit reminded me of Superman.
It ended up being pretty wet up there, so my shoes were soaked and muddy for the entire 32-mile run. This was difficult on my feet because the moist circumstances weakened the skin; I got numerous painful blisters for the majority of the run. This ultra had me hurting

and bruised like I'd never been on a run before. I took up first place about mile 7, while we were jogging on an elk trail and scared a herd. There were new tracks running down the trail, which boosted my motivation. I was completely at ease.

This section of the race reminded me of occasions when I had to race against a herd of elk in the wilderness. I imagined myself sprinting down the trail with my bow, scanning the dense forest for any sign of elk. It was incredible, and I knew that once I passed the guy in front, he'd be a non-factor—a bowhunter racing through some of Wyoming's best elk territory was a tough guy to beat. This portion included a five-mile uphill stretch where the runners behind me could see me from a long distance. I made it a point to pound out this portion as aggressively as I could, aiming to convince their spirits that I was unbreakable.

That Under Armour guy from Oregon is a beast. The race is for second place.

I arrived at the top of the hill with a four- or five-minute advantage after completing the 14-mile stretch. Perfect. I got a few items, took off my shirt because it was becoming hot, and was on my way. The disadvantage of pounding out that section was that my quads and calves were on fire. But I had to be onstage—there were still eighteen miles to go. I needed to pretend everything was well in order to dash the hopes of the guys behind me, who were no doubt seeking for a sign that I was done. Any symbol, such as hands on the head, bending over, hands on knees, etc. My strategy almost worked.

I was the race leader until mile 24 or 25. The issue was that the race did not end at mile 24 or 25. I stopped at an aid station to refuel because I was feeling terrible. I had stomach problems and wondered if it was because of the altitude. I wasn't used to running at 9,000 feet because I lived at sea level. I even ended up hurling a few times after the event. Two runners rushed in, grabbed some items, and left before I could.

There had already been spirits broken in this ultra, but it wasn't theirs.

When you're getting off the couch and out the door, it's natural not to want to travel more into the unknown, knowing that whatever follows next will be more tough. I did this when I first started bowhunting, and I continued to do so when I went backcountry bowhunting on my own after Roy moved. I was now pushing myself even more by jogging greater distances.

Ultramarathons? What on earth was I thinking?

I stood at the entrance, which, as Campbell put it, leads to "darkness, the unknown, and danger." Of course, anything like that piqued my interest. Except for Roy Roth, no one else may comprehend this.

No peak is too high, no challenge too tremendous, and danger is non-existent.

Roy, while not a runner like me, certainly understood the attitude that drove me to compete in the Bighorn Trail Run.

I was prepared.

I started the race with a plan. My plan was to go out aggressively and "break" the other racers by hammering out the first fourteen miles, which featured some difficult ascents (up to 9,000 feet) and harsh descents on game trails. This part had it all: jumping over logs, sliding through mud, and sloshing through snow. I was knocked out twice. Tripping down the steep slopes and flying like Superman, but not really. With my arms outstretched, I was skidding down the hill over pebbles, sticks, and muck. That last bit reminded me of Superman.

It ended up being pretty wet up there, so my shoes were soaked and muddy for the entire 32-mile run. This was difficult on my feet because the moist circumstances weakened the skin; I got numerous painful blisters for the majority of the run. This ultra had me hurting and bruised like I'd never been on a run before. I took up first place about mile 7, while we were jogging on an elk trail and scared a herd. There were new tracks running down the trail, which boosted my motivation. I was completely at ease.

This section of the race reminded me of occasions when I had to race against a herd of elk in the wilderness. I imagined myself sprinting down the trail with my bow, scanning the dense forest for any sign of elk. It was incredible, and I knew that once I passed the guy in front, he'd be a non-factor—a bowhunter racing through some of Wyoming's best elk territory was a tough guy to beat. This portion included a five-mile uphill stretch where the runners behind me could see me from a long distance. I made it a point to pound out this portion as aggressively as I could, aiming to convince their spirits that I was unbreakable.

That Under Armour guy from Oregon is a beast. The race is for second place.

I arrived at the top of the hill with a four- or five-minute advantage after completing the 14-mile stretch. Perfect. I got a few items, took off my shirt because it was becoming hot, and was on my way. The disadvantage of pounding out that section was that my quads and calves were on fire. But I had to be onstage—there were still eighteen miles to go. I needed to pretend everything was well in order to dash the hopes of the guys behind me, who were no doubt seeking for a sign that I was done. Any symbol, such as hands on the head, bending over, hands on knees, etc. My strategy almost worked.

I was the race leader until mile 24 or 25. The issue was that the race did not end at mile 24 or 25. I stopped at an aid station to refuel because I was feeling terrible. I had stomach problems and wondered if it was because of the altitude. I wasn't used to running at 9,000 feet because I lived at sea level. I even ended up hurling a few times after the event. Two runners rushed in, grabbed some items, and left before I could.

There had already been spirits broken in this ultra, but it wasn't theirs.

CHAPTER 8:
BELIEVE TO ACHIEVE

My performance recounted below precedes Mystic Mac's comment, but his approach is exactly what I attempted to mimic in 2008.
"Believe it, then achieve it."
This comes to me as I notice him near mile 7 of the Boston Marathon. He's wearing a gold jersey and is in the middle of a large group of runners.
He's right there. He's the one.
I ran my first Boston Marathon in 2008, fulfilling a long-held ambition. What marathoner does not wish to run the Boston Marathon? I was pleased when I found out that legendary American cyclist Lance Armstrong would be competing in the marathon as well, and I told my kids about it.
"I'm going to find Lance in Boston and run with him for a little while," I told Tanner and Truett. "Perhaps someone will photograph us. I only want one. And then, if I still have any energy left at the end, I'll push as hard as I can to sneak over the finish line just ahead of him."
When I said this, my kids laughed and grinned.
"You actually think you can beat Lance Armstrong?" Tanner inquired.
We'd watched him dominate the Tour de France on TV for years, so the boys were aware of his superhero status.
"You're just a dad," Truett clarified. "He's Lance."
I could understand their scepticism.
Lance Armstrong was an endurance racing icon and legend. He was an Olympic medalist, seven-time Tour de France champion, and the greatest endurance athlete of all time when he started running marathons.
He was not only my hero back then, but practically everyone else's as well. It was one thing to perform on the bike, but his greatest claim to fame may have been surviving a potentially lethal form of testicular cancer that had spread to his lungs and brain.
I did another race with Lance a few years before, in 2006, this time in the New York City Marathon. I completed the 26.2 mile course in 2 hours, 50 minutes, and 21 seconds, averaging roughly 6 minutes

and 30 seconds each mile. I overtook Lance at the one-mile mark that time and never saw him again. As someone who looked up to Lance and enjoyed watching him race in the Tour de France every year, I was ecstatic to defeat the greatest endurance athlete of all time. Of fact, there wasn't actually a race between us, but everyone knew Lance and wanted to pretend it was.

Lance was training hard by 2008 and was truly coming into his own as a marathoner. He ran a marathon in preparation for Boston quicker (2 hours and 46 minutes) than I have ever run for 26.2 miles. His objective for Boston was to break 2:40. Race day in Boston is Patriot's Day, the third Monday in April, which, in my opinion, rendered the 2:40s too ambitious for me at that point in my year's preparation. I was coming off show season, and plenty of travel makes logging mileage tough. Plus, I'm merely an Oregon backwoods bowhunter four years Lance's senior. The mathematics don't quite add up for my fantasy to come true, but that won't stop me from imagining what might happen. I noticed Lance considerably ahead on the line with the elite runners at the start of the Boston Marathon. There were hundreds of people between us, so I had some catching up to do. But I was feeling fantastic, more confident than usual, and after seven miles, I had Armstrong in my sights. It was impossible for me to believe.

I came up to his group and adjusted to their speed. I was starting a little slower than usual, but I always start too fast, blow up, and end up scratching, clawing, and aching like hell just to finish. I'm not a shrewd marathoner. Lance's pacers were keeping him at a steady pace. I figured they, unlike me, had a strong approach.

Around mile 14, we began to encounter some hills. Lance's pacers had vanished, but he was still pounding the pavement. He was a beast climbing the hills. I couldn't possibly keep up with him. I was in a lot of pain and began to beat myself up.

I can't believe I had the opportunity to run with Lance and now I'm letting him pull away.

Leaving me behind with the crowds of runners. Faceless and nameless strangers.

I'm out of options. Nothing.

Hopefully, someone snapped a photo of me with him along the road.

This was one of those critical moments in life when we had a choice to make. When we must choose whether to give up or continue.

Lance was all too familiar with such situations, as he described in his 2000 book, It's Not About the Bike: My Journey Back to Life. "Pain is transient. It may endure a minute, an hour, a day, or a year, but it will eventually fade and be replaced by something else. However, if I leave, it will last forever."

I was about to throw in the towel, thinking I had given it everything I had. Self-doubt began to creep in.

I focus on his calves pounding away in front of me.

Why couldn't I have become an Olympic competitor? Why couldn't I have possessed such talent?

I'm just like everyone else. Some days are difficult. My body hurts, my spirit is shaky, and my head is foggy. It would be much easier to go home and relax during those times, but I never do.

I always show up and work hard. So that's what I'm going to do.

Armstrong once told CNN, "I believe that the mind powers the body, and once the mind says we want to do it, then the body will follow."

This is what I want. I'm going to give it my all. I'm going to track down Lance. If I puke, pass out, or whatever, I'll at least go down in flames.

I increased my pace as much as I could to try to close the distance. My legs had little snap and felt heavy, but by God, I was catching up. Sure enough, I began to feel a little better. It was impossible for me to believe.

I was back on Lance's tail just in time for the course's most difficult hills. He powered them up, leaving me behind a little, then we crested and I caught up, since it appeared that I could run down the hills faster than he could. We were about 19 miles into our journey when Lance asked me a question.

"Was that Heartbreak Hill?"

"No," I reply. "Heartbreak is still a few miles away." Mile 21."

"Then what the hell was that?"

I had no idea, but it stung.

"How are you feeling?" I inquired as we went steadily together.

Lance exclaimed, "I'm fucking dying!"

Thank God, I reasoned, since I, too, am dying, but this offers me hope. Misery enjoys company.

We stayed together, or close, exchanging a few short comments back and forth as the miles ticked by. Running became easier after that. I had definitely caught a second wind.

"Hey, I've lost my pacers," he explained. "How fast are you going to run today?"

"Probably 2:50," I answered.

"I'll just stay with you if you don't care."

"Yeah, that's cool."

Understatement of my life.

The fans were loud. Amazingly loud and almost deafening. They saw Lance coming and went crazy. He had been one of the most recognizable faces in the world at the time, which had people in a frenzy. At the water stations, each volunteer excitedly tried to be the one to hand Lance a cup of water. I heard fans lining the course, yelling, "Lance!" 10,000 times as we ran through the city. It was surreal. I ran beside a legend, beside someone who'd inspired millions all over the world. That man overcame so much. He stared death in the face and battled back to be the very best. It was a beautiful day in Boston. For the last few miles there was a motorcycle with a cameraman on the back, filming every one of Lance's steps. Fans were reaching out, and I wondered if it reminded him of the Tour?

As we came around the corner nearing the finish line, I told myself, Well, here we go. Lance had his own finish line and tape to break for the cameras, so we drifted apart. Then I delved deep and submerged myself in the pain. Amazingly, I ended up coming in twelve seconds ahead of Lance. My time: 2:50:46.

After the race, there was a moment when Lance pointed at me. As bizarre as it sounds, it felt like we sort of created a pseudo camaraderie while running the marathon. I pointed back, then headed over and shook his hand, telling him it was an honour to run alongside him. Not sure he'd even remember me, but I'll never forget that day and that unique marathon. After the race, I raced out to the airport to get back to work the next day. I was excited to talk with those at home about the race. After checking in at the airport, I dug my phone out, listened to voicemails and checked emails. I was overwhelmed. I couldn't believe how many people had seen the footage of me and Lance racing together. After the elite men and women were done with the race, the major story was Lance, so the camera was locked on him—and me—by default. The most welcome of all the voicemails came from Tracey. My wife's voice was heavy with passion as she talked.

"Cam, I am watching you on TV right now and I can't believe it. You are going stride for stride with Lance, and I just want to tell you how good you look, how powerful you are running, and how happy I am of you. I have tears welling up in my eyes watching you, because I know how hard you have worked to do what you are doing right now. Call me."

It's still the loveliest, most heartfelt message I've ever received. I stood there in the bustle of the airport, absorbing every single word she uttered, shaking my head thinking what a lucky man I am. Later on, Tracey told me that Truett, our youngest kid, quietly sat on the couch and watched me on television with a big smile on his beaming face, not saying a word. I learned later that Tanner and Truett's school delivered an announcement over the intercom that their dad ran alongside Lance Armstrong in the Boston Marathon, and beat him. Truly a fantastic day. That happened in 2008, when Lance was a sports god and the entire world adored him, including myself. Prior to the doping scandal, public outcry, and everything that ensued. Did any of this make me reconsider running the marathon with him?

Certainly not. Here's how it works. It's all over. Lance paid the price for his wrongdoing. He was stripped of his victories, forfeited millions of dollars, and suffered further humiliation. It felt weird to be running with him for the entire second half of that marathon. It was also a privilege. Everything that has come out about him after then has not tainted my memories of jogging with Lance. That was also around the time I started getting chastised for putting too much focus on mountain hunting training. That criticism is still there, but it has no bearing on the amount of motivation I have to best prepare my body and mind for the test that is bowhunting. I recently saw the ESPN documentary Lance and thoroughly enjoyed it. I realise everyone has a different opinion on Lance, but despite his difficult history, he was and still is a transcendent symbol in my eyes. It's probably because of my age and where the "Legend of Lance," who was once regarded as the "greatest endurance athlete of all time," fit into my life. Lance still has the same fire inside him, as I saw in the documentary. I'm still a fan.

Visualise your achievement. I've discussed it with regard to bowhunting over the years. Bowhunters achieve their goals by expecting success, working relentlessly to succeed in crunch time, and delivering nothing less than your absolute best. Everything is feasible. The goal-oriented hunter can make his or her dreams a reality. Every fall, this reality is demonstrated time and again in the rugged mountains of the West. I put the visualising hypothesis to the test during the Boston Marathon. Runners and hunters have a lot in common. Many of the same characteristics are required for success in each discipline: commitment, devotion, and, above all, damn hard work. Endurance sports such as marathons and ultramarathons take this devotion to a new level. Similar to backwoods bowhunting. You can train for a 10K by running a few miles three days a week. It's not that difficult. To run a marathon, you should run five or six days a week, averaging seven to ten miles per day, with long runs of up to twenty miles on occasion. That's the allure: there's nothing easy about it. Easy rarely leaves an impression. Similarly, wilderness bowhunting is not something you can do on the spur of the moment. Many have attempted and failed. However, for those who have raised their expectations of themselves in the mountains, tailored their training to utilise every ounce of their potential, and eventually found success, it is a tremendous experience to say the least. Life-changing for some. All I have to do is look in the mirror to see what I'm talking about. For many years, a 10K was the furthest distance I'd ever run. Then I purposefully matched the intensity of my off-season training to that of my hunts. I had high expectations of myself in the backcountry, and I decided that the best way to prepare for the arduous challenge of mountain bowhunting would be to put myself through hell training in the spring and summer. "Cry in training, laugh in battle." That pretty much summed up my newly defined approach to bowhunting success back then.

One of the reasons I admire Lance Armstrong is that he understands the preceding phrase. I really like what he stated about training and determination.

"I'm not happy unless I'm doing something physically painful, like going for a bike ride or running," Lance told Time magazine. "First and foremost, it's excellent for you. Second, it helps to clear my mind on a daily basis. It's also a job. It's my job to suffer. I make training as painful as possible so that the races are not as painful."

Lance not only worked hard in the gym, but he was also a ferocious competitor. "No one trains like me," he declared after winning his fifth Tour de France in 2003. Nobody rides like I do. This is my jersey. This shirt is my life. This is my life. Nobody can take it away from me. "I own this fucking jersey."

Lance did not simply imagine success. He also imagined himself crushing his opponents.

That is a mindset I admire. My father was the other person who praised my race in Boston that day. Because I had always felt like we had a connection through track and field, Lance Armstrong's participation in the Boston Marathon was a delight for him. My father understood what it meant to make sacrifices and strive to be the greatest. He was thrilled to see me on TV jogging beside the icon. He had never really given me credit for my hunting up to that point. As I already stated, he claimed that every time I murdered an animal, I lost brain cells. Instead of receiving recognition for my outdoor excursions, I was frequently rejected. Running was unique. He now had something positive to say about me that he could share with others.

"You know ... my son beat Lance Armstrong."

This was far more fascinating to my father than telling him about the biggest buck I'd ever killed. Lance was well-known to everyone. It was amazing just to participate in an endurance sport alongside him.

As I already stated, my father was my only hero as a child. My pride was high now that I had officially defeated America's hero.

I liked how The Oregonian newspaper referred to me and Lance in the marathon as "Bowhunter."

The headline read, "BOWHUNTER BEATS ARMSTRONG." That is precisely how I prefer it... I'm just a bowhunter, nothing more, nothing less, and I'll stay that way till I die. What do the Boston Marathon and bowhunting have in common? Everything. Oh, I can hear the chorus of guys repeating the same tired statement again and over.

"You don't need to be able to run a marathon to kill with a bow."

I concur. You don't need to do much to kill animals with a bow, but one thing I do know is that the better form you are in, the higher your chances of remaining emotionally and physically devoted to your bowhunting goals. I've been infatuated with mountain bowhunting for so long that I believe the comparisons and similarities I've come up with are valid and worth sharing. In terms of progression, mountain bowhunting, in my opinion, is not that different from other performance sports such as basketball, football, and running. I believe that the ultimate performance pursuit, bare-knuckle bowhunting, is evolving and progressing in the same way that those other sports are. Professional football players wore leather helmets a few decades ago, and I recall seeing an old NFL locker-room photo in which the players looked like they could have been talking politics or, at six feet, 175 pounds, insurance salesmen discussing the benefits of higher deductibles. Compare it to current photographs of NFL players. They're monsters. They rewrite the record books with ever-increasing abilities and no leather helmets, thanks to their solid muscle and track-star speed. Basketball is the same. Have you ever seen old footage of Bob Cousy dribbling and shooting a basketball? I have, and I don't recall ever seeing him use his left hand to touch the ball. No offence intended, given he was The Man in his day, but his shot reminded me of my wife's when she's out shooting hoops with our boys. Yes, the game has evolved significantly. Running, same thing. Every few years, almost every single running record is broken. Men and women are running faster and farther in my favourite sport, ultramarathon running, every year. Similarly, yesterday's legends in bowhunting may struggle to stay up with today's hunter athletes. And there are some archery snipers out there these days.

Please allow me to clarify: Bowhunters in the backcountry are athletes, but they encounter hurdles that other athletes do not. Most sports have rather straightforward training and goal-setting procedures. Sprinters practise to improve their speed. Weight lifters work out to become stronger. The objectives are clearly specified, and the outcomes are easily measured and tracked. And the cheering crowds validate the effort.

I want to give up at some point throughout every long run, and the same is true on difficult bowhunts. "No más!" I've wanted to scream several times. I'm not a superb hunter or a world-class archer. My ability to suffer distinguishes me. I enjoy every minute of bowhunting, but I've yet to go on a simple backcountry trip. As a result, I train like a professional athlete. I practise bleeding.

Some people like to spin what I say as "Cam says everybody needs to be able to run a marathon or they won't be able to kill an elk." I've never stated anything quite similar.

Pay attention... What you do is irrelevant to me.

This is how I feel and what I find works for me. Does that imply that everyone should do what I do? No way.

You can do whatever you want. Do whatever gives you confidence, makes you feel good, or makes you feel empowered. Shoot your bow if that's what you want to do. Go ahead and play chess if that's your thing. Do something that motivates and inspires you. People that give their all every day encourage me.

Those folks think the same thing I do: that anything, and I mean anything, is possible.

CHAPTER 9:
TRAIN HARD, HUNT EASY

"Cam, can't you just do the 50-miler?"
Tracey mentioned this to me as I was about to embark on my first 100-mile mountain run in 2009. I couldn't believe I was only a few days away from the Bighorn 100, which will take place in Wyoming's rocky Bighorn Mountains. The Bighorn 100 was one of the most difficult 100-mile foot races in the United States, with nearly 17,000 feet of elevation gain. It would be my first ultramarathon over 50 miles; the previous year, I finished third overall at the Bighorn 50. It would also be the first race in which I would have to run at night. A full day of running followed by a full night of mountain running sounded, among other things, scary. My wife was having second thoughts and tried to convince me to change my mind.
"You could do really well in a 50-miler," she told me. "You won't have to run at night, but your message will still be delivered." And I've read that on those insanely lengthy runs, people can suffer from kidney failure."
She made some strong points and almost got me a couple of times, but I fought back.
"I've already done a 50-miler," that's what I said. "My goal is to find out exactly what I can do, to find where my breaking point is."
Soon after this chat, my father called me late at night with the same kind of concern.
"You don't have anything left to prove, Cam." Nobody cares whether you run a 100-mile race."
"But, Dad, you're mistaken. I know that not many people will ever do a 100-miler or set it as a goal, but the standard it sets may impact many men. Guys who are tired on their normal run may think about my event and the hardships it entails and find themselves pushing even harder to complete their training." I'm aware that this type of influence works both ways. The tales I hear from folks who follow me on social media motivate me to be the greatest version of myself every day. I am grateful to everyone for their encouragement and for sharing their experiences of bowhunting success and personal growth

with me. Of course, there are the usual suspects who offer opposing viewpoints.

"Cam is a complete moron. "Why on earth would anyone have to run 100 miles to bowhunt?"

That is an excellent question. As I've previously stated, my response has always been: You don't. I don't have to do it, and no one else does either. I just knew I wouldn't be where I am today if I didn't push myself. Conventional wisdom held that twenty minutes of exercise every day, three times per week, and shooting at forty yards a couple months before season would suffice. Such a program does not raise eyebrows, does not question the status quo, and does not make other guys uncomfortable by raising the possibility that they could do more to prepare?

The "norm" wasn't enough for me or many other males who hunt the tough West at this point in our lives. Getting out of your comfort zone and discovering what you are truly capable of is akin to a spiritual awakening. I know I'm a different person than I was twenty-five years ago, and I owe it all to pushing my limitations, asking more of myself, and raising my pain tolerance in the sake of hunting. I'd rather stop hunting than go halfway in preparation. It's all or nothing for me. I was all set for the Bighorn 100. This is only for today. It was only one day in my life. For one day, I can do anything. If I can further deconstruct myself, this is the moment to do so. I went back to bed for a few hours before getting up with Trace to eat breakfast and read the newspaper. I was finally able to leave the house. My intention was to go to Hayward Field for the Prefontaine Classic, where some of the world's most elite athletes were competing and my father was officiating the jumps. I arrived there, nine miles into my run, just as the meet was wrapping up. Seeing such world-class athletes always inspired me. I'd been going to the Pre since I was in elementary school, sometimes simply peering over the fence because I couldn't afford a ticket. The electricity from the meeting had reached me long before, and it did so again on Sunday. I was running down Hayward when I remembered Pre's words, "To give anything less than your best is to sacrifice the gift." I was pumped as I hammered my way up the sidewalk from Hayward. I drove by my grandmother's house and was reminded of how much I missed her since she died. I'd spent a lot of time here, listening to the roar of Hayward, which was only a few blocks away. I accelerated up the steep incline of a street just beyond Grandma Heloise's house. I leaped down the back side of the hill, via Amazon Park, by South Eugene High, to Skinner Butte Park, where Tanner met me on his Trek to ride home with me as I ran. Tanner wanted to help me get home faster since the boys wanted me to take them to Will Ferrell's Land of the Lost. It was genuinely beneficial. With a little more pep in my stride, I pushed through the final five miles of my 20-mile run. "Dad, you seem to be in a good mood," Tanner observed.

I was. On my final prep weekend before the Bighorn, I had accomplished everything I had set out to do. But this is when my psycho-ness manifested itself. I find it difficult to be content. Ever. I was certain there was an official diagnosis. There was every reason for me to be happy. I expected to feel exhausted after clocking 85 miles in three days, which was akin to running more than a 26.2-mile marathon three days in a row. I'm unable to take another step. The skin was stiff and burned. To be sure, I was tired, but not exhausted. I didn't cause any harm. I expected and desired to be hurt. This would imply that there was no doubt that my great effort was successful. But I didn't feel any pain, so I was upset. This naturally made me want to run even more. After a hearty meal with the family, the boys and I went to the movies. I bought their tickets and treats, escorted them to the theatre, and leaned down, saying, "I'll be right back." I'm going to do that five-mile loop along the river, then come back in, get a Slurpee, and finish the movie with you. I'll be back in forty minutes at most." They were cool with it and weren't at all startled. They recognized me. I went outside on another wonderful running night and ran. It was bizarre since I felt fantastic. My legs felt like I'd done something, but I was still able to step out and run strong. Not lightning fast, but flowing. I was overjoyed. A smile covered my face, the same one I experienced when I was in a zone on hunts. This was the sensation I sought every day. I want to continue. Get another 20-mile run in. Then I remembered the boys who were waiting for me. Looking into the darkness of the theatre for my silhouette. I reminisced on my weekend as I made my way back to them. As it was, I pushed my three-day total to just over 90 kilometres. Everything was going so nicely that I was worried that anything would go wrong. A ruptured Achilles tendon or something similar. I crossed my fingers. I knew I had to overcome the impulse to overtrain in the next twelve days before the Bighorn. I wanted to push it when I was feeling fantastic. Hard.Bighorn, on the other hand, would fight back. Even more difficult.I was psyched as I lined up for the Bighorn Mountain Trail 100-mile endurance marathon. But, to be honest, I was also rather nervous. This was dubbed the world's fourth-toughest ultramarathon. The Bighorn 100 was an out-and-back course of 76 miles of single-track trail, 16 miles of difficult double-track jeep route, and 8 miles of gravel road, with a total elevation gain of 17,500 feet and a total drop of 18,000 feet. That simply meant you were either running up or running down. The course was only partially level. I couldn't help but wonder how far 100 miles was. This was my third year in a straight race in a Bighorn race, but it was my first time doing so at this distance. It was a long way to run in any conditions, let alone in Wyoming's high-elevation Bighorn Mountains.

A hundred miles... That is the distance between Eugene and Portland, Oregon. I despise driving to Portland. Was I really going to run that far? Not on a route I disliked, but on a particularly difficult one? At the very least, I knew I'd be racing through lovely countryside. The race kicked out at 11:00 a.m. under beautiful sky and ideal running conditions. I thought I was running intelligently for the first hour or two, but I wasn't. Too quickly. I was also wearing a borrowed CamelBak, which I had never run with before. Dumb. It began rubbing instantly and continued for 29 hours. That rubbed some hide off my lower back, resulting in bleeding silver-dollar-sized hot patches. I began to doubt my ability to complete the event after only twenty miles. It was 1:30 p.m., and I had just finished a 4,000-foot climb; now we were heading down the large drainage on the opposite side. I was already in pain, and I still had eighty miles to go. I realised I wasn't as tough as I thought I was. The organisers mentioned in the race packet to be prepared for anything weather-wise, and they were correct. We went through knee-deep mud and at least a couple miles of postholing in wet, shoe-soaking snow as the course climbed up and over 9,000 feet in the baking sun. Things were looking up by mile 30 at 5:00 that afternoon. Despite a lot of hammering on my body on the way down, and in spots when it was too steep to even run, I began to feel better. I consumed some calories by eating roughly half of a peanut butter and bacon sandwich. Trace did my packing at home. I had gotten back on track. To tell the truth, I shouldn't have been thinking about time at all. For most people, a 100-mile run is a race against their bodies and minds rather than against the clock. I started feeling bad again around 7:00 p.m. I began the 18-mile ascent to the Porcupine turnaround at mile 48. As darkness fell, I realised I'd made a mistake by assuming I'd arrive at the 9,000-foot-plus aid station sooner because I didn't have any of my cold-weather UA and no headlamp. I was fine until 10:00 p.m., when it became too dark to see. I wandered around in the dark woods and snow, falling every third step. This was not helping my deteriorating mood. I was also cold because the wind was whipping across the ridge. I eventually caught up to someone using a headlamp and rode them into the aid station. The highlight of the race occurred at mile 48 around 11:00 p.m. I ate some soup, put on my cold-weather gear, bandaged my feet, and went back out. The assistance station resembled an infirmary. There were some injured racers there, but the crew was fantastic. I had a nurse apply some second-skin-like material to a handful of blisters I suffered after running for kilometres in damp, muddy sneakers. That made a significant difference. I weighed in (they weigh you to see if you're dehydrated) and checked out fine, so I was back on track. I shed some weight, but not a lot. I flew out of there, determined to make up for lost time. The temperature was in the 30s during the race's 48-mile turnaround. The howling wind, approaching midnight, and terrifying beyond made the Porcupine Aid Station a very convenient location for DNFers. For runners who dropped out, that was the official notation on the race results. DNF stands for Did Not Finish. I saw guys at Porcupine who looked like they were on their deathbeds, definitely tough guys (I mean, hell—they had run 48 miles, the final 18 of which were all uphill for a 4,500-foot gain). Medics are wrapping blankets around them. Many people referred to it as a race at Porcupine. But that wasn't the only place where men left. Runners were sitting at practically every aid station, even the most remote, having turned in their race bib. It would have to be dragged out from the remote outposts on horseback, but that didn't matter. They simply couldn't or wouldn't run another step. I could never picture myself quitting before this marathon. I had a newfound understanding for how far you could go. Not only physically, but also, and maybe most crucially, mentally. I believe the majority of the guys quit because it was too much for them mentally. Granted, some suffered from hypothermia and tiredness, but they lost the war between their ears more than anything else. On that point, I ran with an old boy who was doing his 35th 100-mile ultramarathon. As we went over the mountains, I thought to myself, someone that tough, there's no way he'd ever leave a race. So I asked him, and he confirmed that he'd had to pull out of three 100s over the years.

This has to be one of the most exciting moments in history.

By 2:00 a.m., fifteen hours of jogging had been a new experience for me, and it had not been particularly joyful. It was at this point that I envied those who had a pacer or a crew to help them. Some runners had a friend or family member accompany them on vital sections of the race. I was crewless, which was terrible just now. Tanner had put up a great Eminem mix for me on my iPod, and while his "me against the world" bullshit usually drives me, right now I was just feeling sorry for myself. There were instances when I couldn't even walk. Everything was painful. I was so exhausted. I had intended to run the eighteen miles back to the bottom as soon as possible, but it appeared that I was losing time. Although I was losing the fight, the war was far from done. I ignored the advice in the Bighorn race packet.

"Each runner should be aware of the extremely rugged terrain and difficulty this course presents in order to ensure a sufficiently experienced and trained field of participants." This increases the possibility that participants will be prepared to deal with a challenging course and unexpected mountain weather in order to compete safely in the event. It is critical for participants to be aware of the potential physical and mental difficulties that may arise as a result of their participation in this race. The runners may suffer from hypothermia, heat stroke, kidney failure, seizures, low blood sugar, confusion, injury, falling rock or trees, wild animal or reptile attack, or even death as a result of their involvement in this event."

Before I ran, I thought this was some good old-fashioned hyperbole. It is not the case. This race would teach me a valuable lesson. I could feign my way through 50Ks and even 50-milers, but I couldn't feign my way through a 100. Hundred-mile runs are far more difficult than I gave them credit for. This not only put my physical abilities to the test, but it also challenged my thinking powers. If I didn't have to use any intelligence, I could run and do fairly well. I could run a typical 26.2-mile marathon like Boston, New York, or Eugene without stopping, without thinking, without drinking, just hammering it out. If I had to be clever, it was game over.

A 100 required dexterity. But I wasn't done with the game yet. No, not yet. I joined the race believing that given this and that, I should be able to finish in roughly 24 hours... alluding to my illogical rationale.

Last year, I finished third overall in the Bighorn 50-mile race in slightly under 9 hours. Cool, double 9, add a little to account for exhaustion, and bingo: 24.

Cam, you failed the class.

I finished the SOB 31-mile 50K with 7,000 feet of elevation in under 4 hours. By being consistent, I can cover 100 miles in 24 hours.

Nope. My maths was faulty. There was a significant difference between running for 4 hours, 9 hours, and 24 hours or more. Furthermore, 9 hours was the longest I had ever run in my life, and I had only done it once. Even after telling myself a million times that there was one error I had to avoid, I took off far too quickly. I also didn't eat or drink properly, and after around forty miles, I blew up. I rested briefly at the turnaround before deciding to make up time by returning down the hill to Footbridge at mile 66.

Not so quickly.

I couldn't even walk for a couple of hours. I was nauseous, dehydrated, or overhydrated after drinking so much at the turnaround. My hands were all swollen, I was alone, and the lowest of lows occurred about 3:00 a.m., while I was attempting to descend to the canyon's bottom. I was hurting more than I had ever hurt before in my life. That made my pain worse.

I finally arrived at mile 66 around 6:00 a.m. I weighed in, and I was still down but okay. I ate a pancake and sausage, knowing I still had 34 miles to go and another 17-mile climb up Dry Fork. There were some very steep sections, but I never stopped. There was no way you could run it; the only alternative was to power hike. I ploughed ahead, catching and passing some runners near the Dry Fork aid station. That six-hour trek was easily one of the longest of my life. It was relentless. At 12:00 p.m., I reached mile 82. I was really pumped. Every part of me hurt, yet I kept a smile on my face. Sean M. from Sisters, Oregon, provided me with the following advice: Smiling always helps, no matter how horrible circumstances are. I decided to give it a shot on my next difficult hunt. I was now at 25

hours. My 24-hour target had long passed, but I didn't care. I had readjusted and was now on track to finish in the 20s. I'd finish it even if it took 29 hours, 59 minutes, and 59 seconds. I had 5 hours to complete the remaining 18 miles. So long as my body held up, it seemed doable. That was an issue. I was really parched at this point. I weighed 153 pounds, ten pounds less than my official weigh-in of 163 pounds the day before. I needed to drink some fluids, which was a recurring topic for me during the marathon. I ate some watermelon and a PB&J, talked with a couple bowhunters, said hello to Dennis from Oregon, who had been following me for the past twelve hours or so, and then hit the road. At 3:10 p.m., I arrived at the final aid station at mile 95. I blasted off the hill and down 4,000 feet as fast as I could, but those thirteen miles ached. My right Achilles was behaving strangely. I noticed something was badly wrong with it after the race when that ankle swollen to twice the size of my left and I couldn't walk. In terms of my left ankle, it seemed like a bone was protruding from the top of my foot, which I simply ignored, pressed on, and it felt "better." Could I become a doctor? My right knee had a catch, so if I stopped jogging, I couldn't get back up. I kept remembering a famous saying from Mexican rebel Emiliano Zapata: "It is better to die on your feet than to live on your knees." I knew I had to push through the discomfort. Tanner was waiting for me at mile 95 and ran the last five miles with his grandfather. That-a-boy. I told him I couldn't stop because of my knee and that we only had one hour and fifty minutes to run five miles. That sounded strange. Normally, I could run five miles in under thirty minutes at home. Different era, different location. We took off, running slowly, walking quickly, simply moving forward. Always. That was the only thing I did the entire race, and I owe it to Anne Bonney of Under Armour. She suggested RFP—Relentless Forward Progress—in an email prior to the race. I only stopped once on the race to change my shoes at the aid stations. Tanner and I were joking around. He mentioned he was fatigued after roughly two kilometres of our run together. He was also shocked by how fantastic I was feeling.
Appearances can be deceiving.
At 4:20 p.m., I had completed 100 miles. The official time is 29 hours and 20 minutes. I had run a 100-mile ultramarathon! My first 100-miler belt buckle was awarded to me.

It wasn't long ago that I couldn't imagine myself running 100 miles in the mountains. I was excited about the future. For new challenges, testing, and goals.

Nobody could ever take this away from me, no matter what occurred in my life, the highs and lows. I remembered how I felt when I narrowed my first six-by-six bull.

Naturally, my inner monster tried to take some of my thunder. I had not expected to finish in 27th place. But I was fully aware that suffering and broken dreams were excellent teachers.

You can either get to work and improve, or you may languish.

Only roughly 60% of the confirmed registrants finished the event, and only 34 racers finished in under 30 hours, demonstrating how challenging this race could be even for seasoned ultramarathoners.

Back in 2005, I finished twenty-ninth in my first ultramarathon (50K). From there, I gradually improved my performance on the shorter ultras. Reaching new heights, achieving more, and developing confidence helped me arrive at this point, where I can look back and say, "I remember my first 100." That race taught me a lot."

Bowhunting was similar. I used to desire to hunt huge bulls and bucks and travel to Alaska and other exotic locations and nations. The issue was that I couldn't move from a novice bowhunter to the success I desired in one great leap.

Earn your vacation time.

Improve your abilities.

Develop a skill.

Your dreams will eventually come true.

The things I gained in the Wyoming Rockies that weekend were both new and sad. They were also required.

I am grateful for every moment I spent in the Bighorn Mountains.

CHAPTER 10:
THE BEST NEVER REST

What is conceivable when the shackles of comfort are removed? There are a few individuals who understand what is possible when they move beyond their discomfort, master their anguish, and dedicate their lives to be the best at their craft. They are joggers. Courtney Dauwalter is an ultramarathoner.

"I refuse to give my physical pain any value," Courtney told TheTrek.com's Zach Davis. "I push the discomfort aside, concentrate on anything else, and force myself to keep moving... I kept telling myself, 'kept moving. Keep moving. Keep moving.' 'You're OK,' they say at times. You're alright. You're all right.' If I'm being nice to myself, occasionally I may cheer myself on and repeat, 'You're doing a terrific job. You're doing an excellent job. You're doing an excellent job.'"

They are warriors. Michael Chandler, for example, is a martial arts athlete.

"Life is about saying yes," Michael said in an MMAfighting.com story. "Performance is everything in life, especially in this industry." I've taken every opportunity. I've said yes to the UFC (Ultimate Fighting Championship) at the drop of a hat, thinking, 'Holy cow, this guy's a little bit nuts for saying yes to this, but I love it.'"

They are Olympic athletes. As in Emma Coburn.

"I don't take days off; I probably run nine times a week," Emma explained to ESPN. "I find that running with people is the best way to connect with them." I run with someone at least eight of those nine runs a week, if not all nine, so it's a fantastic chance to catch up with pals. My training partners are like family to me."

They have won. "Think Conor McGregor.""I don't care what people say. Never did I. I almost never do. I told you before the battle that I was the shit, and I'll tell you again now that I'm the crap."

They are fighters. For example, ultramarathoner David Goggins.

"Be more than motivated, more than driven, become literally obsessed to the point where people think you're fucking nuts," he wrote in Can't Hurt Me.

They are anomalies. Legends. Freaks. People who test the limits of human capability. And those are the people I follow, not just on social media, but also in person, into the soaring mountains and searing deserts. Every day, I feel inspired to improve myself in some manner. Usually, that entails just doing my own work. In general, I am preoccupied with learning from experts in their fields, or simply the "winners." There have been moments when I've been fortunate enough to spend time with true legends. In those cases, I've wondered what makes them legendary.

What sets them apart from the rest?

What drives them to the heights — and depths — they achieve?

What distinguishes them as true icons?

I've wanted to crack the code and figure out why they're animals, then use what I've learned on my own journey. If I can learn just one thing that will help me become a better, more successful, consistent, insightful, or merciful bowhunter, then my voyage will have been worthwhile. That, to me, is the purpose of life: to learn, experience, share, value, teach, and develop. I could write a book about the outliers I've encountered and what I've learnt from them. I'll give a couple of my personal favourites. We rarely come across someone who questions societal standards. A person who lifts the curtain and shows the public a new universe of what is possible with physical and mental discipline. David Goggins is just as described, and it is a privilege to call him a friend. In my opinion, he is having a significant impact on those who, like him, grew up with the odds stacked against them. As he put it, "You can be born in a fucking sewer and still be the baddest motherfucker on earth." He is aware of this because he is that. He was a melancholy and overweight young man as a result of a difficult life, but he was the first person of the US Armed Forces to finish SEAL school, as well as Army Ranger School and Air Force Tactical Air Controller training. He is also well-known for his participation in ultramarathons and triathlons. Being around people like Goggins makes me realise that I have so much more to give and that I haven't made enough sacrifices. As he frequently says, most of us only use 40% of our potential. We all have so much more to offer than we realise. When I ran 240 miles, I realised this. After finishing, I discovered that I was truly alright. I felt bad during the marathon, but by the finish I was smiling and saying it was fantastic. So I wasn't even close to finished. That wasn't the end of it. Goggins tests his limits to their utmost. Goggins discusses his tale and offers advice into how anyone may realise their best potential in his violent book may Hurt Me. "A lot of us surround ourselves with people who speak to our desire for comfort," Goggins said. "Who would rather help us callous over our wounds and try again than treat the pain of our wounds and prevent further injury?" We need to be surrounded by individuals who will tell us what we need to hear, not what we want to hear, while also not making us feel like we're up against the impossible."

Goggins inspires me just by what he stands for and the honest, unabashed way he approaches life. Some people may be put off by his attitude. I've discovered that true outliers can make those who accept mediocrity uncomfortable. Goggins, on the other hand, has no time or patience for mediocrity.

"Mediocrity feels so fucking good!" Goggins made a post. "If you don't want to work out when you wake up, all you have to say is, 'Fuck it, I don't give a shit!'" And if you're mediocre, you're probably surrounded by other mediocre people, so they're relieved that you don't add stress to their lives! A big joyful soft-assed family!!! People don't appreciate being around that motherfucker who constantly makes them feel uncomfortable or like an underachiever! We avoid the fucking savage that wakes up at 0330 regardless of the weather, whether they had a good night's sleep, or if their life stinks and times are tough. Keep your distance from that cat! People like that make you doubt yourself. They also show you where your life ends and theirs begins!"

Some people enjoy criticising him, but he is doing it, making a real difference in society, while they make excuses or simply try to dim his brightness. People like David Goggins inspire me because they battle, bleed, and sacrifice comfort every day as they scratch and claw their way to their full potential.

If I see someone who is extremely successful, I will never say, "It must be nice." Rather, I study, ask questions, and learn to see if I can leverage their technique to help me advance. I get excited when I meet folks who are more successful than me. I'm eager to learn what makes them tick. Why are they the best at what they do, and how can I use it to be the best at what I do? I don't waste time being envious or spiteful, or attempting to belittle their position at the top of the mountain and the effort required to reach it. There is also room for others. I realise I'm not a great athlete. I'm hardly the best shooter in the world—I'm sure there are better hunters out there. The difference is that I will not stop. What I'm good at isn't a gift. I'll simply do more and work harder than most people are willing to do. I understand what it's like to be ordinary and identify myself by my constraints, but over the course of my life, I've drawn the curtain back on those who push the boundaries. They are oddities, yet they are still people. We belong to the same species. And now I'm jogging, training, and learning from those crazy people. When you surround yourself with people who are pushing the boundaries, you will be inspired or pushed to go beyond what you thought was possible. It is easier to challenge yourself when you are surrounded by others who share your objective of self-improvement and are dedicated to that goal.

I enjoy commemorating excellence. I crave being among people who have achieved success in their industry and whose attributes I aspire to emulate. I'm always looking for opportunities to rub shoulders with winners in the hopes that some of their greatness will rub off on me. Courtney Dauwalter is one such individual. She is the world's number one female ultrarunner. Her pleasant attitude and grin are the only things that can compete with her sprinting ability. The reality is that I work hard all year to get in shape so she doesn't have to wait too long when we run together.

Courtney's name initially came to my attention when we both ran the Moab 240, which she won. I had no idea I was up against someone The New York Times would refer to as "the woman who outruns the men, 200 miles at a time." I mean... dammit. According to the publication, in the Moab 240, "Dauwalter obliterated the competition."

I can attest to that.

When I went off in the race, I told myself, "You've got to be smart." As previously stated, I am not the most astute runner. In these races, I normally take off far too quickly. I was leading by hours the first day of my first 200-mile race, the Bigfoot 200, but I ran too fast. Then I dried up (dried out) and blew up (faded quickly). So I decided to be careful with Moab and keep track of the leaders, knowing that the race might go several days. I knew I had plenty of time. I recall arriving at one aid station and inquiring who was in the lead.

"Courtney Dauwalter."

"Who?" I inquired. "Where's she at?"

When they told me she was ten miles ahead of everyone else, I figured she had taken the incorrect route.

She can't possibly be that far ahead of us. She had to have missed a turn or veered off track. But no ... Courtney just smashed the 238.3 miles of Moab, winning the race and defeating every male and woman in the field. Joe Rogan was watching to see how I was doing during the race because there was live tracking available to keep track of the competitors. As he did so, he noticed her great performance and thought, "Holy shit, I need to talk to this Courtney." He had her on his show, and that's when I first learned about her tale. That's when a lot of people realised who she was and realised she was one of the best ultrarunners ever. She has won the Western States 100-mile race, the Ultra-Trail du Mont-Blanc ultramarathon in Europe, and the Tarawera Ultramarathon in New Zealand. Courtney is without a doubt a legend. We've had some fantastic trips. One of the nicest days I've ever had was when Courtney and I hiked the Grand Canyon from rim to rim. Courtney knows the importance of mental strength in her sport. "For me, this is the most interesting part of ultrarunning," she remarked in an interview with 2020. "During my first 100-mile attempt, I dropped out around mile 60 because my legs hurt so much and I didn't know how to shift gears to the mental game." When it becomes physically uncomfortable, which is unavoidable, I try to tell myself that by keeping tough in my head, not giving up on myself, and pushing forward, I can psychologically overcome the physical discomfort."

Do you see why I enjoy running with her?

Courtney sought to beat the 490-mile Colorado Trail record in 2020. I ran with her for twenty-six hours during her effort. She looked at me at one point and asked whether I was okay. She had been jogging for four days and asked whether I was okay. I couldn't help but laugh.

"I'm not falling for this shit," I smiled. "You're not asking how I'm doing after running for four days!" You're not concerned about me."

Taking in the dry mountain air continually for days on end at above 10,000 feet elevation dried up her lungs. Her nose was also continually bleeding, but it was the deep, raspy cough that worried her. She's really tough, though, and even though her legs were still strong after 309 miles, she went to the ER, where doctors reported her oxygen level was quite low and she had acute bronchitis. They insisted she not return, and when asked what would happen if she did, the doctor replied, "Well, she could die on the trail."

I've stated that I want to discover my limitations, to see what happens when I push myself too far. Courtney has discovered hers. She's been there at least once. But, given the circumstances, that was her limit; she's not done yet. I'm willing to wager that 309 miles is not her breaking point. Her potential's promised land goes well beyond that. I've learned from her that we can all go far beyond what we thought was possible. She's simply incredible. Outliers understand that your body will sometimes say, "Not this time."

To complete it, your mind, body, and spirit must all be in sync, which is why it is so special when it goes well. It's potent. This life-changing venture is so fantastic that you can't help but want to come back for more, despite the pain of putting it all on the line and the possible heartache of knowing there is a genuine possibility of crashing and falling short. Only a few people return. Those are the people I want to keep looking for and following. Jordan is one of the greatest athletes of all time. Kobe. Brady. Tiger. LeBron James. Wayne Gretzky. Pelé. If you're only recognized by one name, that signifies you outworked everyone else. You became a legend by becoming a zealot. I appreciate the excellent examples. That is what I am most passionate about. I think about athletes like Usain Bolt. Serena Williams comes to mind as an example. People who go far beyond anyone who has gone before them. Superhuman in appearance. Outliers. Freaks. Many people have potential, but only a few are obsessed. Michael Jordan's competitive mentality is something I can relate to. When I was working my way up in the hunting industry, some of my acquaintances said I was "too competitive." They were most likely correct, and I haven't altered a bit. The only difference now is that instead of competing against everyone else, I am only competing against myself. Other than for inspiration, no one else is even on my radar. Unless, of course, they talk smack. And, while I don't believe what the naysayers say, I never forget, which is also MJ-esque. The elite athletes of the UFC are one of the groups that motivate me the most. What do UFC fighters have in common with world-class ultramarathoners and mountain bowhunters? Doesn't this seem like a strange combination? Perhaps, but the common thread is that each profession is exceedingly tough to perfect, and only those who put in the blood, sweat, and tears succeed. There are no shortcuts or replacements for hard work!

Why do I associate folks who are insanely dedicated to a trade or art with my chosen passion, bowhunting, when I listen to them? Conor McGregor is an excellent illustration of this. Conor's every word conveys the mindset of a fighter, a warrior. I hear lessons that a receptive bowhunter could or should accept. Conor understands that you can't talk your way to the top. Conor knows the value of hard effort. When Conor asks, "Who is going out there, time and time again, back-to-back-to-back-to-back, putting it all on the line and continuing to show up?" he could be reading the audiobook to my life's narrative.

"I had to work my fucking bollocks off to get it, and here I am still working," Conor stated in an interview in 2016. "While they're speaking... I'm talking, but I'm walking a whole lot more than I'm talking."

Conor McGregor epitomises a champion's mindset that can be applied to any worthwhile pursuit. I usually declare that I don't have a plan for success, but Conor's story reveals a time-honoured one.

To begin, you must work, sweat, and bleed with unfettered zeal. And you must be completely focused on your craft.

Second, you must adjust your mindset and believe that you are the greatest you can be with every single breath you take.

Finally, like Conor, it is beneficial to have someone in your life that believes in you wholeheartedly and will never doubt you. The sky's the limit with that formula in place.

It's a state of mind. All of the greats share a mindset and a philosophy. Courtney is the one who carries it. Goggins, Michael Chandler, and Colby all agree. I need to understand what motivates them. What drives them? This is what keeps me going. They are what keep me going. I'd like to see if I can advance to the next level. I'd like to see what that looks like. This has been demonstrated to me by these outliers and many others. Emma Coburn has done the same. Keeping up with them has been difficult, especially since Emma is the most dominant steeplechase runner in US history. Nothing beats putting in miles on the trails above Crested Butte with Emma. For the most part, I struggled to keep up with our mountain runs. After seeing her perform firsthand, I believe that her training at altitude, as well as years of trail running, has translated into helpful strength for her expertise. Running at a fast rate while navigating uneven terrain, rocks, and tree roots appears to have improved her inherent athletic power, allowing her to not only go over, but also come off those barriers better than her opponents. Emma won bronze at the 2016 Olympics and performed admirably at the 2020 US Olympic Trials, when she won the steeplechase and set a new trials record. She was disqualified after falling during the steeplechase Olympic final, but one race will not define her. All I can say is that she has mastered her trade. She's a true beast. I recall seeing her do an outdoor mile in Colorado Springs, which is 7,000 feet above sea level. Because there is less oxygen to use, running rapidly for distance becomes more difficult than usual. Emma was near the back of the field after three laps as they reached the last turn. She began to close the gap and pull others in shortly before the final turn. It was incredible to watch. I inquired about the race. I was curious as to what made her click, what drove her to succeed. I knew Emma might have easily thought to herself throughout the race, "Well, it's 7,000 feet." I simply don't have it today. I'm competing against milers, and I'm not one. I ran 3,000 metres. It's not my day. She could have just relaxed in and joined the pack and had a great time. I still ran a 4:30 mile, which is rather quick. She may have also persuaded herself, "It's going to hurt, but I don't care."

There was a point, a decision she made, when she resolved to give it her all, knowing it would hurt terribly. Nobody would ever know. Nobody would doubt whether she gave 85 percent, 90 percent, or 99 percent. Emma cranked it up, overtaking every other female competitor down the line, and won the race. I inquired about the decision she made. What was your experience like? She merely shook her head and stated that there was no decision to be made. This was what she had been taught. She hasn't been schooled to make judgments, such as deciding not to give it her all. She's been prepared to win. This is where my desire to run stems from. I'm going to go running, regardless of how tired I am or how horrible the weather is... I'm going to run. Emma's attitude is fantastic.

"Why?"

It's a common question. In fact, I was asked this question by one of the top athletes in the history of her sport at an Under Armour event a few years ago. Why do I enjoy running so much and so far?

"I know you like pain, right?" she inquired.

I do, but that isn't why I enjoy jogging. In terms of pain, I enjoy it because it shows that I am sacrificing and pushing past where most people would give up. That's the one advantage I've convinced myself I have. The ability to tolerate discomfort. And I'll argue that practically everyone who does 100-mile ultramarathons, as I have, has a very high pain threshold. In extreme endurance racing, pain is unavoidable. I told the celebrity athlete that I enjoy running because it makes me feel invincible to be able to run hard for hours over the mountains. I had the same sensation when holding my bow in front of a grizzly bear, a Cape buffalo, a lion, and so forth. Is it true that I am invincible? Obviously not, but I am in my thoughts, and that is all that matters. I consider myself fortunate. Very fortunate. I understand that it's strange. This guy, who established his name as a bowhunter, is suddenly jogging with these legends. I don't really deserve to hang out with Olympians, icons, and performance freaks, but I do. And I train alongside them. They are the finest in the world at what they do, but I am not one of them as a runner. There are many other people who should be running and training with them. But shouldn't the greatest train alongside the best?

Here's the deal. I don't consider myself to be the best bowhunter in the world. Every year, I feel like I'm on the point of failing. I don't pat myself on the back, nod, and say "GOAT!" when I kill an animal. Instead, I accept the realities.

Cam, you did exactly what you were meant to do. You didn't accomplish much. You're expected to be good by training, hunting, killing, and eating elk. But I'm always second-guessing myself and hearing the demons of doubt until I score that first kill. This could be the year that the rug is yanked out from under the truth. That's why I put forth so much effort. That is why I pursue outliers. I don't believe I have any talent. I consider myself fortunate. I sometimes feel like I've been blessed for the past thirty years. Soon, your luck will run out, the truth will be revealed, and everyone will realise you're a fraud.

All I have...

All I have to offer is...

All I can do is outwork everyone else. Otherwise, everyone will know the truth, and I'll be back where I belong, doing mediocre things and dreaming mediocre dreams.

Every day, I have to put in the effort. And I will never be satisfied.

I can't rely on my innate talent or accept that I've accomplished enough. I can't let myself believe that I deserve a day off. No way. I need to constantly figure out methods to improve, to push harder, to train with others, to learn from them, and to improve what I do. If I don't, this garbage will end. I don't consider myself extraordinary, but there are individuals that look to me for motivation. So I don't want to disappoint them. We must all strive to make a positive influence, since what is the sense of living if you are not working to make one?

The greatest of the best, as well as the toughest of the tough. It's a harsh world full of rough and ragged people battling for the summit of the mountain. So why do I run with the greatest, hang out with outcasts, and train with freaks? Maybe it's because I grew up doing just that with Roy Roth all the time. People would see Roy as this enormous guy, but anyone who believed he was a "average" man was mistaken. Anyone who hunted with Roy immediately discovered that he could outwalk, outwork, outhunt, out problem-solve, and out-tough even the most elite mountain athlete, let alone the average hunter. When people dismissed Roy's abilities by saying things like, "Roy could get it done with a bow and he wasn't a gym rat," I'd always answer, "Yeah, maybe so, but you're not Roy."

Nobody resembled Roy. He was a unique individual. I understood this firsthand and wanted others to know it, which is why I enjoyed writing stories about his achievements. Roy forced me to become accustomed to being among other breeds. Maybe that's why I keep looking for them...Roy is no longer present. I placed it atop Mount Pisgah, and thus a tradition was born. I took it back down Mount Pisgah the following week while running. I resolved to transport the rock back and forth once a week. As they passed me and my rock on the route, people would look at me with furrowed brows and inquire what I was doing.

"Trying to get tough," I explained. Some laughed aloud or merely shook their heads as they strolled away, leaving me to fight with my rock. I began to hear other people's questions and doubts.

"Why would you do that?"

"You're going to get hurt."

"You're going to feel stupid when you drop it on your foot."

And the finest part...

"What a waste of time."

Exactly. I want to do something that no one else wants to do, something that no one else values. That is my sole advantage. I didn't find out how much the rock weighed until after a few journeys up and down over the next few weeks. I brought the boulder to the gym and carefully placed it on the scale after bringing it down one time. It weighed in at 130 pounds. Some may regard me and my rock-carrying exploits as ridiculous or simply stupid, but I enjoyed doing it and overcoming the pain and weariness. Sure, my seventy-pound estimate was slightly off. But when I got up there and carried the rock, I told myself that if I could do it ten times, I'd feel like I'd accomplished something. Fun fact: a video of this levity was one of the first videos Joe Rogan saw of me on my YouTube channel years ago. What is this guy doing with this rock? he wondered. Rogan was fascinated and invited others to join him on the broadcast via Twitter. Since then, we've been wonderful friends. There's an old adage about leaving no stone unturned, about trying every method and action to get what you desire. That's how I feel right now. I practically leave no stone unturned in some circumstances. Uncarried as well. My fitness regimen began to change the moment I chose to get in shape in order to be the greatest bowhunter I could be, and it has developed over time. It's been dubbed Beast Mode, Lift, Run, Shoot, and Train Hard, Hunt Easy. I recall thinking about what it would be like if I spent eleven months of the year running, exercising, and shooting with one objective in mind: to arrow a large bull in September, the month of mountain elk hunting. Was it necessary for me to do this?

I had the same thought regarding the finest athletes of the day. Was it really necessary for Kobe Bryant to shoot 1,000 jumpers per day? Manny Pacquiao needed to run 10 miles every morning, complete 2,000 sit-ups every day, and train like a man possessed for eight weeks straight. Was it really necessary for UFC fighter Georges St-Pierre to do pull-ups with a 120-pound weight connected to his waist and have only 5% body fat? Is it really necessary to run, lift, and shoot every day in order to prepare for mountain bowhunting?

"No" was the response to all of these queries, but I began to wonder what it would look like if all of that stuff was done. So that's what I started doing. I would start the day by running and doing reps before going to work. I'd go for another run at lunch, then shoot my bow and work out in the gym in the evening. I gradually improved my fitness. If you told a thirty-year-old me today about my current

workout routine, he'd reply, "No, that's impossible." But I've just been pushing my body to find the limit of what I can do to give me the ultimate advantage over everyone. That is why I strive to push myself to muscular failure eight or nine times every day. That's why, on days when I don't run a full marathon and instead only run twenty miles, I compensate with an hour of weightlifting in the gym. That's why I allocate up time every day for compound bow target practice. That's why I try to get in as many kilometres as possible... to discover the ultimate limit of where I'm at my best. There are no days off. As ridiculous as it may appear, I don't think I'm good enough to take a day off. And I shall never be. Running, training, and bow shooting have always served as a form of rehabilitation for me. It's my liberation. I've run the mountains with folks who enjoy the challenge or by myself over the years. I've fired bows alone or with individuals who share my passion for archery. I've worked out with my sons or with friends who encourage me to be better, stronger, and more thankful. The more difficult the workout, the happier we feel. What I refer to as my Lift, Run, Shoot lifestyle is a means to an end, which is hunting. Preparation is essential for reaching any objective. You cannot rely on chance or genius; both will always leave you empty-handed. When you push your body and think you've reached your limit, have you really? I trust Goggins when he says that most people quit at 40% of their full potential. But assume you're one of the few who works as hard as Courtney. Pushing yourself too far might sometimes help you become the finest version of yourself. It assists you in identifying your "limit," whether actual or perceived, so that you may gradually learn to push past it and find a new one. There is no substitute for everyday commitment to your art, whatever it is. That means punching the time clock every day, giving everything I have seven days a week, and never being satisfied.
I enjoy being weary.
I enjoy being depleted.
I enjoy knowing that I have nothing else to offer.
That is commitment.
I never grow tired of jogging those kilometres, lifting those weights, or shooting those arrows.
I'm on the route I've always wanted to go.
James Clear summarises the contrast between amateurs and pros in Atomic Habits:

"Professionals stick to a schedule; amateurs let life interfere." Professionals know what is important to them and work hard to achieve it; amateurs are swayed by life's exigencies... When a habit is truly important to you, you must be willing to stick to it regardless of your mood. Professionals act even when they are not in the mood. They may not enjoy it, but they manage to get the reps in."

Dedication fosters atomic behaviours such as this. Being a professional entails doing the essential tasks repeatedly. Do you want to learn how to be a beast? Do you want me to record my everyday routine? Do you want to see how long I run and how many reps I do? Do you want to know my secret? It's already been shared 10,000 times. What I'll say is this. You're not working hard enough if you're not the hardest worker you know. An outlier will never let someone outwork them. That being stated, here are some of my beliefs that fit into my Beast Mode mentality and compete alongside my Lift, Run, Shoot days. This is what I am aware of and comprehend. This is why I continue to hammer. Running alone and knocking out miles is soothing and keeps me focused. Smiling is a good thing, and you can't help but smile when you see the sun rise on those early morning runs. I enjoy working up a sweat in the morning to get my mind in order before heading to work. A few arrows may be more effective than coffee in cleansing the mind. A nice cup of both, on the other hand, is probably best. Isn't reaching the pinnacle always a win? Even on my worst days, I am always grateful to view the monument at the mountain's summit. Spending quality time with my family is a must. Training for misery is the only way to train and discover my limits. Pushing through pain allows you to run when your ankles, knees, hips, or feet aren't cooperating. Lifting weights is something I enjoy doing. I enjoy the pump, the veins, and the burn. I appreciate being sore, feeling strong and unmistakable in the mountains, and looking fit. I enjoy it when people notice me and inquire about what I do.

"What do you mean?" I ask.

"I mean, why are you in such great shape? "Are you preparing for something?"

"Yes. Bowhunting."

I enjoy it when all of my hard work pays off.

The most crucial aspect of lifting is to concentrate on the reps. Weight is unimportant. It all comes down to repetitions and stamina.

Shooting a bow looks cool and gives you a sense of power. Shooting bows with friends is a unique experience.

Every day shooting is required. Sensing pain indicates that you are sacrificing, and sacrifice positions you for a large return. I've discovered that your body will do whatever you ask of it. Humans are incredibly capable of accomplishing so much. Push yourself to the limit. For me, hunting is the ultimate. The goal is to become ready for the first hunt of the season. Pushing myself harder each year allows me to become more and more prepared. When you're in Beast Mode, you feel like you're in a superhuman state of being, as if you're playing at a higher level than everyone else. Is this true? It makes no difference. You are what you believe you are. A winner's mindset is unbeatable. This strategy, I feel, equips you to be prepared in the woods, to be ready for "crunch time" when you release the arrow you've been picturing at the animal of your dreams. This type of training teaches you that there are varying levels of discomfort. The idea is to get used to it by doing weight training and running. I'm uneasy, but I still feel at ease. I'm out of my element, yet I'm still capable of succeeding. I can keep my cool while hunting by simulating tiredness and creating misery. It reminds me that I've been here a million times before and that I'll be fine, make good decisions, and do what I'm here to do. I get it done by doing all of this for decade after decade after decade. There was a comical TV advertising campaign in the 2000s that featured events that always finished with the same catch phrase. One commercial depicted an operating room with a surgeon surrounded by nurses performing surgery on a patient.

"How's everything look?" the surgeon inquired.

"Looks good," said the nurse. "Looks really good."

"What's his BP?" he inquired.

"One twenty over eighty," stated another nurse.

"OK, folks, close him up," the surgeon said as he removed his surgical mask.

A nurse was taken aback by his appearance. "You're not Dr. Stewart."

"No," he responded casually as he started to walk away, then added, "but I did stay at a Holiday Inn Express last night."

The commercials concluded, "It won't make you smarter." However, you will feel smarter."

When I'm asked specific questions about my workout, diet, or anything else relating to my training, I think of those commercials. I feel like any advice I give should be qualified with an asterisk, as in, "No, I'm not a fitness expert, but I did stay at a Holiday Inn Express last night!"

That is why I do not offer counsel or reveal some imaginary plan.

I'm not a fitness professional.

I am not a bodybuilder and do not intend to become one. I lift in order to become a well-rounded hunting athlete. I'm not a powerlifter, but I have a lot of respect for the guys who are... The people at the local gyms here in town teach me so much. I try my best and am always learning and perfecting my skill, but I am not a fitness expert. I am not a physician. Otherwise, I wouldn't do the idiotic, risky, health-threatening things I do. Before you try anything, consult a doctor if you have any questions. All I am is a bowhunter attempting to raise my game to the highest level possible. In this regard, I feel that the only limitations we have, both physically and intellectually, are those we impose on ourselves. You will succeed if you believe. My method works for me, but it does not ensure that it will work for others. I'm not even the best archer, but I'd like to be. There are better shooters at my local pro shop, the Bow Rack, than me, but I work extremely hard at it. The key to my success is to put in the effort in all I do. Because I can't scout elk every day, I have to lift, run, and shoot. No, I did not spend the night at a Holiday Inn Express. I slept outside in the wilderness, waiting for my hard work to pay off. I fell asleep, knowing there was nothing else I could, should, or would do differently. Today, I'll have to play the cards dealt to me and see what occurs, but whatever cards I have, I'll use to win the hand. This is the attitude I bring with me to the mountains. To be aggressive, hunt wisely, and return from the hills laden with meat and antlers.

Understand your worth.

Normally, I'm bad at this because I'd bowhunt for free. When money is involved, it tends to dilute the genuine impact bowhunting has had on my life as a man. But I can't be stupid, and I know my worth, therefore that deserves respect as well. My family relies on me to make sound judgments because I use those decisions to improve their quality of life and secure their future. In the name of my family, I've exploited my value as a bowhunter to pay for private schools, college, automobiles, and mansions. I, for one, don't require anything. I'm absolutely content with my shithouse, shitcar, and the regular nine-to-five job I still have; my wife and kids are likewise content. But I know that if I can invest in their education, it will lead to additional opportunities, or if I can pay off their car and truck loans, they will be able to focus on success rather than expenses. Keeping this in mind, I just negotiated a new deal with one of my favourite sponsors, Hoyt, the manufacturer of the bow I use. I was underpaid and knew it, but I didn't care for years because money doesn't motivate me. However, when it came time to sign a new contract, I was determined to be more serious about my worth, because if we don't advocate for ourselves, how can we expect others to? I stated that I needed more money because I knew I was underpaid for what I provided. They claimed they would quadruple my current contract, which I thought was excellent but still insufficient. So they offered to quadruple it again, putting me in the six-figure range for work I'd perform for free. But I had to be smart enough not to do it for free. The other side of the coin is that I worked hard for Hoyt for many years and earned their trust. I'm fortunate to have a sponsor like them who, in addition to financial help, has always believed in and supported me. Even at four times what they paid me last year, my goal is to remain their greatest value. My goal is to work so hard for the people that pay me, whether it's my normal job or my sponsors, that if things get rough, I'd be the last one let go. Ten times a day, I'm asked on social media, "How can I become a professional bowhunter?"

"How can I get sponsored?"

"I'd like to do what you do... "Can you assist me?"

No, I am unable to assist you. Only you can assist you. Everyone seems to want to be noticed these days, so I constantly ask the same question: "What are you doing to set yourself apart?"

I'll meet youngsters who want to be in hunting publications, have their names on bows, and have their own shoes, and they'll ask me how they can do it. They don't understand. It's difficult to put into words. All of that came after the adventure was completed. After all those long, alone, unseen hours alone trying to do what I love.

"Do you enjoy shooting your bow?" I always ask them.

"Yeah," they might respond.

"All right, then shoot your bow." A lot. Practice shooting your bow. "I'll worry about the rest later."

You can't create a hunting footwear without first destroying a few pairs. I often tell people to make sure their path is fuelled by their passion. If you don't enjoy running, don't set the aim of becoming a great marathon runner. It will not work unless you are passionate about it.

This happens occasionally at my 9-to-5 employment. "How do I get your job?" guys will inquire.

"Why do you want my job?" I inquire.

"Because you make good money," they explain.

"Well, if your goal is to make good money, then it's not going to happen," I replied.

That is not the case. Money will come if your purpose is to improve, to push yourself, and to assist others in succeeding. If money is your ultimate goal, it's unlikely to work out. It's simple to watch the advertisements, movies, and stuff and then tell these young kids or authors, "I want to be a famous bowhunter."

That's not a very good goal. Do you want to be a celebrity or go bowhunting?

The goal should be to become the best bowhunter possible. To discover how to sacrifice, go on the best adventures, and live life to the fullest as a bowhunter. If you really want to go hunting in the bush, even if you don't have the time or the resources, you'll find it out if it's important to you. I'll say it again: my way is not the only way. It's all mine. Your path to success may be very different, but I'm sure it will include hard effort and sacrifice. I guarantee you that everybody you look up to in any field works their tail off and has a winning attitude. An elite running athlete does what everyone despises: runs intervals, pushes themselves, possibly pukes, eats perfectly, and sees their vision as destiny. An outstanding businessman outworks his peers by creating reports, crunching figures, and leading by expecting dedication. An exceptional construction foreman understands the big picture, plans ahead, and keeps his workers engaged and motivated. These folks do not grumble or seek an easy way out of their jobs. They put themselves and others on the line by lifting the bar. Get to work if you want to succeed in any sector, even the hunting industry. And remember to smile because every day is a gift. Respect that gift.

CHAPTER 11:
THE FICKLE WINDS OF FATE

Do I have a right to be here?
For decades, I had fantasised about hunting on the San Carlos Apache Indian Reservation. San Carlos, located in southeast Arizona and comprising 1.8 million acres of land, produces what I think to be the most incredible elk in the world. As a lifetime elk hunter, carrying my bow in quest of the country's greatest bulls in these majestic mountains was a blessing and a dream come true. The dreamlike experience was something I never expected as a young bowhunter from Oregon thirty years ago when I had so little money. I never considered going on an out-of-state elk hunt back then. Because concentrations are low and this country is managed for prize bulls, the reservation only allocates a few tags each year. This implies that hunting there is prohibitively expensive. A hunt like that costs upwards of $70,000, which is more than I've made in a year for virtually my entire life. Compare that to the $1,100 tag on my first out-of-state elk in Wyoming!
My motivation was the hunt for a gigantic bull and adventure in fabled territory, but money was a concern. I recall when this initially became a source of stress for me. When I was editor of Eastmans' Bowhunting Journal in 2005, they took me on a premium Colorado elk hunt that was videotaped for the TV show. The $10,000 price tag came with the quest. I was having trouble getting the expense out of my brain and focusing on launching a perfect arrow. On such a hunt, if you take a bad shot and draw blood, even if the shot isn't fatal, that's your animal. I worried that I'd mess up, blow the shot, and Eastmans' would have to sign a check for $10,000 with nothing to show for it. I ended up hitting the biggest bull I'd ever killed, a 350-inch six-by-six. He ran fifty yards and died in seconds after I shot an arrow through his lungs. I've always put a lot of pressure on myself to make a clean kill, but having money resting on my performance in crunch time increased the intensity even more. Some of the top elk hunts now can cost four times the $10,000 Colorado elk hunt. I quickly realised that hunting prime countries is a business. Because the animals are valuable to outfitters, when you go on a hunt like that, you must sign a "wounding policy." As I previously stated, this

formal agreement states that if you draw blood on an animal, it is yours. It makes little difference if the hit is lethal or if you only graze the animal and he rushes away, never to be seen again. You own every drop of blood that falls to the ground. I knew I'd never seen a ten-by-nine bull in my life until hunting San Carlos for the first time. I had no idea that was a thing. And a 400-inch bull—I'd never seen one in the wild before. To go after a bull of that calibre? It wasn't even a plausible fantasy for me. Chris Goode, our guide, showed me a video of the bull when I arrived at camp. I could only remark, "Incredible." Chris had recently recorded this footage via his spotting scope and stated that the ten-by-nine was dwelling in steep, tough terrain. He thought it would be ideal for me to locate and stalk this bull. This is how I've dispatched 90% of my bulls. Kip Fulks, one of Under Armour's early creators and a personal friend of mine, was there with me, and he was the one who gave me this opportunity in San Carlos. I was confident as I walked out into the best elk habitat in the world for two weeks if necessary, but the idea of getting a chance at a once-in-a-lifetime bull like this seemed absolutely unrealistic. I didn't even spend much time imagining the prospect. Instead, I persuaded myself that even if I could arrow a 380-inch bull, it would be more than enough. Such an animal would be more appropriate for someone like me. Chris had different plans. His target for us was a 400-inch bull. To be honest, in that country, a 400 bull is always the aim. That is their standard. I nicknamed the ten-by-nine-foot beast "Tight Bull" because he was so skinny. What were the chances of locating him? After all, the reservation covered 1.8 million acres, it was big territory, and the rut was in full swing, so the bulls could be anywhere and on a hot cow. We had some near contacts but no can't-miss possibilities after a couple days of elk hunting that included around ten miles of hiking, calling, glassing, stalking bulls, and so on. We heard what sounded like a good bull bugling, responding to Chris's cow calls, one unforgettable evening as we made our way up a hill through a burn. The wind was quartering up the hill from left to right, so I knew we needed to be at or slightly above where the bull would emerge from the timber at the burn's edge. Kip, Chris, and I raced straight up through the burn as fast as we could. We set up when we were around fifty yards above the bull. I leaned against the shadow side of a large burned oak, searching the tree line closely. Chris and Kip were about forty yards behind me, over a small spine crest. So far, so good.

The unnoticed bull screamed a bugle. He was almost there. I calculated his exit point from the woods and looked for shooting routes. It was a shambles. The fire had left charred trees and foliage everywhere. I became concerned that if he entered the burn, I wouldn't have a clear shot. I had only a few seconds to make a decision. At the moment of truth, a bowhunter makes crucial decisions that impact success or failure. The line between the two is razor thin. I glanced at the tree I was leaning on and found some decent limbs to climb. I quickly guessed that I'd improve my possible shot opportunities if I climbed up the tree. Since I had been set up on the shady side of the tree, my movement would be considerably less obvious in the shadows. Scaling the tree as swiftly as I could, I ascended ten to fifteen feet up and set up to shoot. This elevated position freed up my shooting paths substantially. Seconds after being placed in the tree, the bull ripped a bugle, replying to Chris and displaying himself. It was the Tight Bull thirty yards away! While we were in his country, we had no notion he was the bull coming in. I took one quick glimpse at his 400+-inch, ten-by-nine rack, understood what bull he was, and put my emphasis on getting a decent arrow in him. Chris cow-called and Tight Bull closed in, moving straight for me and then halted directly underneath me. I carefully retracted my bow. The bull grew frightened when he observed movement or sensed or heard me—probably thinking "mountain lion" if you could have asked him—and ran back toward the timber. He came to a halt at just under thirty yards, quartering away as I desperately tried to get into shooting position while balancing on a charred tree limb fifteen feet up an old burnt snag. The Tight Bull stood there, staring back at me, trying to figure out what was going on. I needed to act quickly. My sight was set to thirty yards, which would suffice, so I quickly readjusted while remaining cool. I placed my sight pin on his vitals, but there was one small limb hiding his breast, so I rose to my tiptoes in the tree and chose a location.

It had come down to the wire.

This is the most important moment for a bowhunter to master, as adrenaline rushes through your body and your heart accelerates. Success will be difficult if you are unable to maintain control. If you're good at it, releasing a perfect arrow is merely another step in the process. If you've worked hard, you'll look forward to crunch time since it's your chance to shine. Bend that bow back, anchor in, choose a spot, and launch a razor-sharp broadhead. The arrow flies toward the bull and lands exactly where you expected it to, because you've worked too hard to fail. You spot your bull after following a brief blood trail and humbly kneel beside the beautiful animal that gave its life for you. The bull's memory would be honoured when his antlers graced your wall and his flesh fed you. I swiftly aimed an arrow at the largest bull I'd ever seen. On release, I felt confidence in the shot, confident in the work I'd put in, and confident that the arrow would land exactly where I'd imagined it would. That would have been ideal... but that is not what happened. The arrow grazed the bull high and to the right, grazing the top of his shoulder blade. A high, far-ahead shot on a big bull is about the worst shot you can make since it's high and forward of the lungs, which is where you want the arrow to hit. Because the bull is protected by strong muscle and bone, an arrow that strikes here will usually merely hurt the bull rather than kill it. As he rushed over the ridge with what appeared to be half my arrow protruding from his shoulder, I felt sick to my stomach. How did I squander an opportunity that I had spent my whole adult life preparing for? In the fraction of a second it took my arrow to leave my bow and strike the bull, my fantasy turned into a nightmare. For me, a hunt evokes a wide range of emotions, including thankfulness as I am immersed in nature's beauty and reverence as I move among predators and over terrain that can take a man's life in the blink of an eye. It serves as a reminder to all who pay heed that death favours no man. When the heavy senses-muting garment of the civilised world is flung off the shoulders, there is also a heightened sensation of awareness. Finally, the hunting instinct might take over. This sense returns to me more quickly each season, as my years in the mountains have now turned into decades. However, killing with what is essentially a sharp stick is never a guarantee. Because man is primarily a visitor to the wild, animals have an advantage in the wilderness. But we have reason and knowledge on our side, which allows us to reach inside bow range if we hunt properly and the wind holds. If our aim is steady and our timing is correct, that "sharp stick" will strike our quarry and kill it. He'll sprint a short distance to his last bed.

We do our best to honour this event with words and photographs from the huge difficulty we conquered in a harsh country. We talk about respect, we honour the animal that fell victim to our arrow, and yes, there are bittersweet feelings when you've accomplished your hunting goal as an animal lies dead at your feet. We believe that death is a part of life, and hunters accept that in order for humans to exist, animals must die.

To be honest, I'm not concerned with the size of antlers, as many men are. They call it trophy hunting. I'm not worried about trophy size, but I do want an old animal. I want an animal like the Tight Bull that has served its purpose, has been bred, has done its job to help the herd survive, and is now effectively past its prime. That's what I'm after. This is when months of training, running, and weight lifting pay dividends. I trust my ability and my equipment to be accurate and focused. My primary concern is to do everything possible to achieve a precise shot that rapidly kills the animal. It's a big relief when I do. If I cause an animal to suffer, I will suffer mentally for many years. I understand that hunting and the death of an animal are difficult concepts for some people to grasp. Even after decades of hunting, the actual death of an animal is not something I like. Achieving my aim and fulfilling my life's purpose? Yes, that is satisfying, and I recognize that as a bowhunter, success means the animal dies. I'll deal with the blood on my hands because it means elk meat will be feeding me, my friends, and my family for months. Nothing, as we all know, lasts forever. An ancient bull may live to be 10 or twelve years old. I've killed people as old as fifteen. Even so, dying in the wild would be far more drawn out and agonising if not for a perfect arrow, and I take solace, even with its emotional baggage, when I can offer a beautiful death of an animal I admire like no other with a perfect arrow.

CHAPTER 12:
LEGENDS NEVER DIE

"The mountains never lie."
On September 30, 2015, I shared this quotation on Instagram, along with a photo from my recent Alaska moose hunt, and discussed how, while humans lie and we even deceive ourselves, the mountains never lie.
I don't kill if I'm not in form and emotionally prepared for a tough hunt, like my Alaska moose trip last week. On that hunt, there was a lot to overcome: severe weather, grizzly running off bulls, dense fog that reduced visibility to nothing for the majority of the hunt... just the regular backcountry hunting challenges that one experiences in Alaska's highlands. But when you're exhausted, cold, out of food, and unable to see, it doesn't take much to force you off the mountain and back down to the comforts of town to lick your wounds. The mountain will tell you how strong and prepared you are at moments like this. Because the mountains never tell the truth. Personally, I live for the mountains' rough love. Four days after I posted those sentiments online, the mountains would question my strength and readiness to confront the severe scars that life could offer. They'd dish out that rough love, forcing me to face an ugly truth: my spirit was frail, my heart might shatter, and my faith could fade. The confidence I had worked so hard to create didn't just crumble. It collapsed. Some mountain ties are so powerful that breaking them feels like losing a piece of yourself. "What's up?"
Roy called to check in on me at work.
"Oh, you know, just in my cubicle," I blurted out. "It's insane here. Doing purchase orders is really thrilling. Being on the mountain, arrowing bulls or bears, and packing meat is ten times better. Much better!"
"Oh, that sounds really fun," Roy responded.
"How about you?" "Are you living on the precipice today?"
"Well, I went to Home Depot and got some light bulbs."
"Seriously?" I pretended to be excited. "That sounds insane."
"But wait until you hear this. I had to return because I had ordered the incorrect ones. That was quite intense."

We shared a giggle about our dreadfully uninteresting day. Not only did I get to have so many incredible hunts with Big Roy, but I also got to enjoy those ridiculous talks. They were always a means for us to check in with each other, to banter and reconnect, to chat about previous hunts, and sometimes just to remind ourselves that we were still there for each other. Always. Our previous hunt together had been a gruelling moose hunt in Alaska only a week before. I had to make a ninety-yard bow shot, and then we had to transport all the moose quarters from deep in the mountains four kilometres away. We matured as bowhunters and men from that difficult hunt, just as we had from all the others. It was one of the most memorable backcountry hunts we'd ever done together. The moose hunt had followed an amazing bear hunt, which we didn't think we'd ever be able to top. I arrowed two large wild country brown bears for camp meat—one a nine-foot six-inch monster boar, the other a seven-foot boar and a good-looking black bear. We were living life to the fullest. Roy would be off to the Dall sheep mountains in another week, while I would be in Colorado chasing rutting deer. Roy had asked if I wanted to go sheep hunting and filming with him, but I already had my deer trip planned. We planned to stay in touch with nightly phone calls when reception permitted. I was eager to return to the wilderness with Roy. Our previous two hunts had been fantastic. Roy had demonstrated his toughness and strength, as well as his conviction in our ability to succeed, on each one. I had asked him how long he thought it would take me to get a good bull killed with my bow before our mountain moose hunt in-country, which was actually a rifle-hunting area where success was far from certain.

"What do you think, three days?" I inquired.

"Yeah, if that," Roy responded confidently.

On the third day, we were closing up on a bull I had bedded down earlier that day, and it was my first true stalk of the hunt. Roy stared at me from a couple hundred yards out, with a million things that could go wrong to spoil a challenging bowhunt, in awful circumstances with swirling winds, and stated, "Dude, it's gonna happen." I responded, "I know, buddy." That it did. Roy's confidence sprang not just from his belief in what was achievable, but also from his refusal to blink in the face of peril. This happened during the brown bear hunt we went on earlier that year in July. We had difficulty with a large brown bear. She spotted us from about 130 yards away and began running full speed at us. I knocked an arrow while Roy prepped his .375, which he'd packed as backup. I'm not sure what an arrow would do to a charging brown bear, but it was the only weapon I had. He said, "If she gets to our side of the creek, I'm going to have to shoot her."

She ran toward us after crossing the water without hesitation. She came to a halt some twenty yards away, huffing and looking us down, her head swinging side to side. We were standing in the open, in knee-high grass, so no one could mistake us for animals. We were giving her a second opportunity since we didn't want to kill her unless absolutely necessary.

"Get out of here," we screamed.

It didn't make a difference. The brown bear lowered herself to the ground and charged, her ears pinned back. Roy shot her once and stoned her at close range. We're only a few feet away. I couldn't stop myself from saying a loud and improper foul word.

"Fuck."

I was furious that we had to slaughter yet another bear. I'd already killed a nice boar, and we were buzzing from our fantastic success and the cool footage of my perfect bow shot. We now had another person slain, which we did not want. Despite the fact that we were in terrible danger, the thought never occurred to us. Roy remarked matter-of-factly after I cussed and shook my head, "Dude, I had to."

"I know, it just stinks," I said.

"Oh my God, we could have been killed, are you okay?" would be a normal response. "I'm trembling." But I was familiar with Roy, my companion. He had the same level of assurance that I did. He was never shaken and was always in command. I knew I'd never find another mate like Roy in ten lifetimes. Where do you get your strength? Muscles can only be grown by doing something that tears them down, then repairing themselves to answer a test and repeating the process. Bottom line: You get what you ask for from your body. My workout routine involves a 1.5-mile run up Mount Pisgah, a local hill with a 1,100-foot elevation rise. I can do this several times every run and get in a lot of leg and cardio work. I also lift weights and spend time shooting a bow every day. To gain endurance and strength, you must be disciplined. Something else propelled Roy. In a book he personalised to me years ago, he once described where his power came from.

Cam: Seasons pass us by. This is the only constant in my life.

Roy jotted this down in a Bible he handed me. His religion remained constant over the decades I knew him. While I was all over the place, he remained rock solid. Jill was his only girlfriend, whom he adored and married. Before settling down, I took a different route. He never used a curse word in his entire life, but I did. He never drank alcohol, although I used to drink plenty for both of us. Despite being diametrically opposed in many ways, our relationship never wavered, not even slightly. We were united by our love of bowhunting and the strength we brought into the forest. Not only was Roy a terrific bowhunting partner, but he was also a man I could always count on in times of need, someone I could tell anything to and never be judged. Despite the fact that dad had always been a devout Christian and I had not, he never "preached" to me. He exhibited pure life, which I aspired to, and he always answered my inquiries about his ideas. Roy not only enjoyed bowhunting, but he also enjoyed knowing that he was able to influence people he would never have met otherwise.

"I believe the hunting world is my mission's field," Roy commented once. "You can't just walk up to a bunch of people and say, 'Hey, you know, this is what I believe.' This is how I believe you should believe.' They have zero regard for you. You must gain respect in order for others to listen to you and for you to make an impact on them. And the hunting world is a harsh one in that regard. So, if you can acquire their respect through your hunting achievements, I believe God gave you such abilities."

I was in Colorado bowhunting with Kip Fulks and Marc Womack a week later, now weeks after our moose hunt. I noticed and stalked a large Colorado whitetail as the sun fell over the eastern plains. He was in pre-rut mode and had just watched another ten-point, so he was tense. While Kip was hunting elsewhere, Marc and I were pinned down.

"I'm just going to go for it, try to cut the distance down by about 100 yards," I told Marc, who was recording me.

I moved as softly as I could approaching the deer. He noticed something a few times, but I was largely crawling and remaining low. We assumed he mistook me for the other deer, so as I drew in on him, he began charging my way. He came quickly, licking his lips, and even stopped to scrape the sage brush. I thought it was time when he started to skirt me at sixty yards. The shot felt terrific, but it was a little low and he was quartered to a small degree. I decided it was good enough to murder him, so Marc and I retreated, intending to return at first light to retrieve him.

We watched the tape before going to bed that night and came to the conclusion, "dead buck." It appeared to be liver, but you never know. I climbed into my bed that night, excited and confident that we would find the deer the next morning. Sleep, on the other hand, refused to come. My cell phone rang around 11:00 p.m. Trace was the one.

"Roy's been in an accident," she explained.

She didn't know everything that had transpired, so I realised I needed to call Roy's wife, Jill. I called her and inquired as to what was going on.

Jill finally remarked, "Cam, Roy's not coming home."

Jill's voice sounded tired and quiet.

"What do you mean?" I inquired.

"He fell," she explained. He had died."

My stomach fell, and the darkness of the ancient farmhouse kitchen in the middle of nowhere, Colorado, felt darker and more lonely. I couldn't believe what she said.

I immediately thought of their children, Taylor, Justin, and Ellen.

Roy had died after falling 700 feet from a precipice in the harsh terrain where we hunted sheep. He was on Pioneer Peak, the same peak where I killed my ram in 2008 and where Roy has killed rams ever since. The mountain had won in 2015.

He lost his footing while performing something we'd done many times before in the type of country we liked to hunt in. Tough, rough, and merciless. Colt Foster, a fellow hunter, was with him and witnessed the tragedy. They eventually had to fly in a helicopter to rescue Roy's body. Jill's husband had died, their children had lost their father, and their company had lost its heart and soul. It was catastrophic.

I stayed up all night, heartbroken, angry, and perplexed as to how someone I thought was invincible in the mountains could have a fatal accident. When the alarms finally went off and the others awoke, I informed them of the situation while we waited for the sun to rise. They sipped their coffee while I sat there staring, tears welling up in my bloodshot eyes and rolling down my cheeks. We went out when there was enough light to look for my buck. That morning's hunt for the buck was excruciating. I had a few good men on my side. Instead of remaining with the others after the initial failed effort, I went out by myself, inspecting the ground while crying and looking for blood. I ran into the other guys every now and again, so I tried to keep my eyes dry while we asked each other, "Anything?" That is, any indication of blood.

"Nope" was the response each time.

I was so desperate to find this deer for Roy that it hurt. However, hunting can be a frustrating experience at times. I knew the buck didn't care about Roy and wouldn't risk his life to offer me a shred of happiness to compensate for the anguish. Roy, on the other hand, I know would have delighted to see my deer and hear a good hunting story. I had to track down the buck for Roy. We all swore to keep looking until we found him, because Roy and I had always agreed on difficult blood traces. We'd get him if he died or was about to die. And we always have. However, the lack of a blood trail in this country meant that the journey would be difficult. I remembered Roy and how he had recently obtained his outfitter's licence. We had grand plans. We'd spent decades establishing a brotherhood while chasing Alaska's most epic bow hunting excursions, and things were finally clicking. Everyone wanted to hunt with Big Roy, therefore Roy's outfitting business was booming. He had grand plans to go on this fantastic caribou and bear combo hunt. We were both thrilled about the future since becoming an outfitter would provide him with additional opportunities to experience authentic Alaskan adventure. Everything looked to be falling into place for Roy.

Life will never be the same again.

I imagined how Roy might have reacted if he had learned such news about me. I knew he'd be tough as nails. On the other hand, I couldn't have felt weaker. I was upset that we wouldn't be able to go on another hunt together. I was sad because I would never again be miserable in the mountains with him, which was one of our favourite activities. My heart went out to his family. Roy's idea, or perhaps it was his advice, eventually guided us in the right way, and the grid search paid off. We discovered "Roy's buck" dead after he ran about a mile from where I hit him the night before. My GPS tracker showed that I'd gone six kilometres looking that morning, and the other guys—Marc, Kip, Sean, and Tom—had done the same. I owed them all for their perseverance in the pursuit of Roy's buck. He was a lovely animal, and the meat was as tasty and fragrant as ever. I was grateful for it. To me, the Colorado whitetail deer I had killed would always be Roy's buck. More tears poured as I called Jill and told her it felt like Roy was among us, assisting me in getting my buck. We had maintained our "Roy tough" demeanour, and it had paid off. Roy's memorial service was lovely, poignant, and uplifting. Many of those in attendance, I believe, received God's love in the midst of their suffering. Roy had everything he desired: his family, Palmer High School (where his children attended and where he coached baseball and football), hundreds of friends, and legions of strong Alaskan hunters much like him. Roy set the benchmark for which many of us aimed. The enormous throng demonstrated the community's regard for Roy. He had made an impact. He inspired people to accomplish more, work harder, be better, and love more deeply. But I believe Roy would have appreciated the Lord's great presence the most. The sadness of Roy's death was palpable for everyone during his memorial ceremony. What I intended to do was to be strong for those who were suffering more than me, such as his wife, Jill, their children, his mother and father, sisters, and so on. However, as I stepped behind the podium, I discovered that talking about Roy in the past tense was more difficult than I had anticipated. I didn't have any notes and hadn't really thought about what I wanted to say. I just wanted to say what was on my mind. That's what I did. But there was still no way for me to really convey how I felt. How could I appropriately summarise Roy's introduction to my life's passion and subsequent many adventures with me?

How could anybody know that, as a child and young man traversing a dysfunctional household tainted by alcoholism, I had finally found peace in archery, with Roy as my anchor and best friend?

How do I even begin to describe Roy's unwavering faith in me and my dreams? Not only do I have bowhunting dreams, but also writing and business dreams. In Roy's mind, no challenge was too great. Nobody could ever grasp it like I did. We believed we could succeed with our bows in any situation, and we did for nearly 30 years in some of the most harsh, brutal, untamed land.

I felt like I failed while I was onstage speaking at his service. Jill saw me in pain and felt inclined to come up and hug me as I spoke about what Roy meant to me. When I went and sat down after speaking, I was hard on myself.

Wow, way to screw that up.

While it would have been nice to be a little more composed, I later felt that maybe I had achieved my goal of conveying the impact Roy had had on me after reading a message a gentleman sent me on Facebook.

Hi Cameron,

I wanted to tell you how much I valued what you had to say about your friend. Your words about friendship and love and faith and doubt were so raw, so real. I think we are all accustomed to pleasantries and platitudes, where emotion from the heart is watered down into trite phrases, but you offered only honesty. "I sure loved that man. I think he loved me, too ... Some days I believe I'm going to see him again, but there are other days when I just don't know ...

I was crying. I think everyone else was, too.

What really struck me from the service is how much Roy impacted those around him. I've gotten so used to hearing packaged sermons and haphazardly sprinkled Bible verses, but Roy was the gospel for the people in his path. The way he lived his life and chose to love those around him, including you, was an example for everyone who knew him of what a life in communion with God looks like. I'll leave you with one more thought I've been dwelling on. All of the "Roy stories" I have heard over the years, including your words about your dear friend, tell of a big man who lived a big life. And now, partly because of Roy's impact on your life, you have chosen to share with people a glimpse into your faith. Maybe that means you are the gospel as well? Maybe I can be the gospel, too?

I couldn't answer that man's question, because I didn't know. It was just another chapter in the saga of my own meandering path through friendship and love and faith and doubt. Roy Roth was the toughest person I've ever met. I sometimes find myself unfairly comparing others to him and then I remember: There will never be anyone like Roy. But the second-toughest person I've known might be his wife, Jill. She was strong at his service, and she has remained strong. Soon after Roy's passing, Jill set the goal of creating a room for Roy, which would include some of his mounts, mementos, photos, and so on ... all things Roy. With the help of friends, family, and Roy and

Jill's kids, Roy's Room was completed just as she envisioned, two years after his death.

To celebrate the unveiling, Jill organised a gathering held at their home, and it was amazing. Roy's Room was filled with so many good people, which included Roy's mom, dad, sisters, children, grandchildren, hunting buddies, fellow coaches, and friends from church to name a few. Stories flowed freely. It was just the type of crowd and conversation Roy loved and it all happened because of Jill and her loyalty to Roy. I am honoured to have known Roy and call him my best friend, and similarly I am honoured to know, love, and respect Jill. She's not tough in the mountains like Roy was but she's just as tough in her own way. Her strength and poise in losing Roy has amazed me. Just like Roy, Jill leads by example. I could write a book about Roy's toughness and optimistic outlook, and maybe one day I will. One story I'll never forget is our Dall sheep hunt in 2008 on Alaska's gorgeous and steep Pioneer Peak, which was beautifully recorded on film. The lines I wrote in my story about the hunt appeared to predict what happened to Roy exactly seven years later in the same country, on the same type of bowhunt. The ascent to sheep country is arduous and one I won't soon forget...

I'd been anxious about this hunt since the beginning. I was fully aware that this might be the only sheep hunt I'd ever embark on in my whole life...

Make no mistake: if you got into trouble on the mountain, no one in the valley could help you. Regardless of the viewpoint, Alaska sheep country is an unforgiving region. As many have observed, I suffered a severe hit on my ram during that sheep hunt. My arrow bounced off a boulder I was trying to avoid and struck him in the ankle. It essentially severed his wrist. He made it up and over the mountain while we kept an eye on him the entire time. The sheep was bleeding, but no one wanted to shoot an animal. I climbed up to where Roy had witnessed my stalk and the shot from after witnessing him go over the top. As the ram limped up the mountain, he, too, noticed the blood on its ankle.

"Nice shot," Roy remarked as I approached him.

I looked up at the rocky ridge the ram had vanished over. "Yeah, cool, isn't it?" "I stink." "We'll get him. We might have to wait a week, but we'll get him."

"Yep," I answered, nodding.

That kind of attitude and steadfast confidence meant a lot. Those who have viewed the video will know that we eventually got him. It was a harrowing experience: I had to catch the not-quite-dead-yet ram before he slid off a cliff and hold him there as he died, but we got him. That hunt will always remind Roy that, despite his fearlessness, he understood the dangers of those mountains. The same country that eventually claimed his life. I think it's important to convey the counsel Roy gave me as I was heading down to finish off my sheep, because while he had earned his confidence, he wasn't stupid or reckless. My ram was perched on the edge of a cliff in icy and snow-covered terrain. "Well, I have to go get him," I remarked, peering over the ridgetop at the crippled ram. Roy examined the cliff. "I'm not sure if you can even get down there, Cam, where he's at." And if you do, you may not be able to escape."
"Maybe so," I answered, looking down at the frail ram. We'll have to wait and see."
And I was off. That day, fate was on our side. I approached the ram, killed him, and we escorted him down the mountain. In the same situation today, I believe the conclusion would be identical, but the victory would not be as sweet as it was then, since I shared it with Roy, the one person on this planet who understood what killing that ram meant to me and what it took to get it done. I believe he felt the same way about me because whenever he did something "next level," I was his first call. When he poked his head into the brown bear lair and the ten-foot bear swiped at him as it boiled out, he contacted me from the mountain minutes later, excitedly telling me the story. When he killed a large Doll or a giant grizzly, which he had done more than any other bowhunter in the world, I'm sure he'd call and say something like, "Too hard." Because this was "code" for us, I'd jokingly feed into the game and say, "Well, that's okay, it's just good to get out in nature." Roy, you don't have to kill to have a good time.``
We'd laugh, and I'd generally say something like, "So, now that we've gotten the jokes out of the way, can you get it done?" He'd always respond, "Cam, that's why I went."
Yes, Roy was always on time.
"When the chips are down, what gives you strength to keep pushing?"

When I asked Roy this question, the first thing he said was his deep Christian faith. Just like on my Dall sheep hunt, he was confident that everything would work out according to God's plan. He consistently maintained an optimistic attitude and expected to achieve his aim on each and every hunt. Roy believed that God had given him the power and ability to succeed, which would allow him to have a beneficial influence on others.

In terms of my religion... I'm still struggling.

When someone passes away, everyone says, "They're in a better place" and "We'll see him again." People talk about how wonderful Heaven will be, and it all sounds lovely. It makes you happy. But my faith isn't completely unshakeable. I believe, and some days I feel well and believe I shall see Toy again. Then there are days when I wonder.

In 2015, we had high hopes and ambitious objectives. We'd enjoyed two of our best hunts and were looking forward to Roy receiving his outfitter's licence. Because of his nice attitude, hunting skills, and ruggedness, I felt Roy would make the best outfitter ever. Things were going well until he died. To be honest, I'm still upset about what occurred. But I'll never forget what Jill told me about Roy's death. It comforts me in the same manner that I'm sure it comforts her.

Jill was understandably unable to sleep the night she discovered Roy had died after falling from his balcony. She awoke around 1:00 a.m. and gazed out the window. Pioneer Peak could be seen from their house, so Jill looked up to the mountain Roy had died on as a glow appeared over it. Jill recalls seeing a brilliant light.

Jill described it as the Lord saying, "Don't worry about Roy Boy." Tonight, I'll be keeping an eye on him."

She was aware that she was not sleeping and dreaming about it. Jill told me that she knew things were going to be okay at this point because she felt a sense of calm wash over her. Hearing that made me happy. I wish I could have witnessed it for myself. When I think about Roy, I still don't feel at ease. That is not what is in my heart. Because of the weather, the rescue crew couldn't get Roy off the mountain until the next morning, and they only had a few hours before another storm hit. When Jill got the message that Roy's body was on its way in on the helicopter, she and the kids headed to the Palmer airport to wait for him. The tragedy became real for Roy's family at that point. I tell Roy whenever I have a nice hunt or a good year. That's what we always spoke about: our accomplishments. His success was my success, and my success was his success. Roy was concerned about me, and he shared my interests in bowhunting, challenges, doing things no one else would, and living on the edge.

I've always admired Big Roy's unshakeable faith, and I desire for the same assurance he had in eternal life beyond death. He was irreplaceable as a presence in my life, but I'll persevere, keep pounding, and do my best to always commemorate Roy Roth's legend.

CHAPTER 13:
THE INVINCIBLE IMPOSTER

I'm unbeatable.

My alarm is set for 4:55 a.m. because getting up "in the fours" sounds more committed to me than getting up "in the fives," but I never make it to the alarm. I switch it off before it turns off.

I don't fear getting out of bed; in fact, I enjoy it.

It's another opportunity to hammer.

I've convinced myself that every day is a gift, and that I should get out of bed and go for a run. I'm generally out the door before 5:00 a.m. to begin my fastest cardio run.

In my head, I prefer running around the deserted streets and seeing the houses with everyone asleep inside. I don't envy them because I feel that every morning is another opportunity to make a little more sacrifice. I turn it around and think about how I'm already out there working. That makes me happy.

According to the adage, the bigger the sacrifice, the greater the reward.

This has always been true.

This will always be true.

You can second-guess, cut corners, and reject, but you can never change the game. When you modify your positive effort, the chances shift in your favour. That is a proven fact.

There is never a doubt in my mind about whether or not I will run today. I'm going to run regardless. I'll run even if I'm unwell. If I'm hurt, I'll take it easy. I'm going to limp. Nothing is going to change. Many people hunt for excuses not to run or exercise. Those thoughts no longer cross my mind.

If I think I'm exhausted, I remember running hundreds of miles in an ultramarathon and only getting an hour or less of sleep. That's when I should be exhausted. The rest of the time, it just means I'm weak.

Even though I've killed a number of bulls, upwards of sixty in my thirty-plus years of bowhunting them, and had more than my fair share of success, none of that matters this elk season. That is what drives me to work every day.

I think about it a lot when I'm among people who are outstanding in their fields. Who succeeds because, like me, they work their asses hard, but they also have far more God-given talent than I to focus on their craft. They have Olympic-level talent, tunnel-visioned intensity, and an extraordinary level of tenacity and mental power. They will succeed because their ability and work ethic are both exceptional, which is what distinguishes them as living legends performing at a level that many have never witnessed. I only achieve because I work harder, because I get up at this hour every day and hammer it out. This level of training has given me tremendous confidence in the mountains. The more I sacrifice and suffer in training while pushing toward my objective, the more lethal I feel with my bow. Is it excessive? No thanks. I've discovered that you can never prepare too much. Every year, every hunt, every day, you learn something new, but you have to make sacrifices to keep the education going. So you want to go bowhunting? Do you wish to compete in ultramarathons? That kind of nonsense doesn't happen overnight. You must work on it every day. You must continue to sacrifice, sacrifice, sacrifice.

There will be a payback. But it will take some time.

Tomorrow is never certain. I could have tremendous hopes and goals in the future, but I could also die tomorrow. So I basically take each day as it comes. Every day, I give it my all. I'm a forger.

When I look back on my life, I wonder what the hell happened and how I got here. I think about where I came from, what I've accomplished, and how many things I don't deserve. I think about the hunts I get to go on, the people I meet, and the lives I get to change, and I sometimes feel like someone is going to break into my house and shake me awake.

"What in the world is going on here, Cam?" What exactly are you doing here? What do you make of this? Return to your dingy little village and the dingy life you deserve."

There are moments when I believe that will occur. I've mentioned it to Joe Rogan previously, and he says he sometimes feels like that because of his background. Here's a regular guy who just landed a gigantic $200 million podcast deal and is experiencing what specialists call "impostor syndrome," or the feeling of being a pretender in your life. I understand. I'm the superintendent at work, but I don't feel like I deserve to be there. The guys look up to me, and I'm skilled at managing men, but I'm not sure I deserve to be superintendent. I don't have a college diploma. I never requested the position of superintendent. I was the buyer, and I was quite excellent

at it. My friend was promoted to director, and I knew he needed help with the field people, so I offered to help. It's not like I ever imagined myself as a superintendent, especially with everything else going on. So I didn't know back then, and I still don't. Sure, I know I make a lot of sacrifices, but I also know that other individuals make a lot of sacrifices and don't get the same rewards that I get. I am humbled when individuals post comments about how I improved their lives. I don't believe I deserve that kind of power. I'm honoured to have it. I feel unworthy when I think about all the individuals I've let down, disappointed, and failed to show sympathy for when I should have, or when I've been selfish when I should have contributed. It bothers me. When I was running one day, I was listening to this podcast and hearing folks say things like, "Cam gets to go on some pretty sweet hunts" and "I can't afford $70,000 for an elk hunt like he can." What are you talking about? I ask myself. I can't afford it, and neither can you! I'm lumped in with the rich folks, but in my mind, I'm still thinking I'm just this warehouse worker because someone will figure out this charade and I'll be back there. "Hey, can I get some overtime?" I'll say as I'm working back in the warehouse. Because I'd be generating a substantial amount of money over time. Because if you're making ten dollars, you're suddenly making fifteen dollars at a time and a half. That all adds up. That is significant. That is still my mindset. People who put me in some higher category or preconceived box understand, but it is neither who I am nor how I feel. Maybe that's why I never feel like I've accomplished enough. Why do I feel I have to make more sacrifices than everybody else? Maybe it demonstrates that, okay, this is why I have everything, this is why I'm blessed. It's because I'm more generous. I think I'll die before I feel like I've made it, like I've arrived and can relax now. The drawback, if there is one, is that I don't believe what I do is a recipe for a long life.
I'm completely smitten.
I advise people to be focused or average. Obsession is often required to complete tough jobs.
I was so preoccupied with tagging a bull with my bow when I first started bowhunting that I skipped all of my college classes, missing the first two weeks of school, until I arrowed that bull in the middle of September. I wouldn't have missed an entire month if I hadn't gotten him. That much meant a lot and still does.

Things pique my interest. But, as I often say, if you aren't obsessed, you will be mediocre. It doesn't matter to me. Nobody will ever know your name if you have a good, balanced relationship with whatever dream you have. That is the harsh reality. Sure, some people are born with the physical abilities to play in the NBA, but LeBron James would probably say he's been obsessed with basketball his entire life.

The legendary Wayne Gretzky once stated that parents would approach him and ask him if he could tell their sons how many hours a day he practised hockey.

"I say, I didn't," Gretzky explained. "It was a labour of love." I could spend all day out there because I enjoyed it."

If you want to excel, you must think about it, obsess about it, and sacrifice, or it will never happen. That's the end of it. Bowhunting became my obsession. That's the end of the narrative.

It's not the end of the narrative, though. Every day, with hard work, the story continues. Because of obsession.

Jerry Rice, one of the finest players to ever play in the NFL, used to run up a hill. In fact, it's known as "The Hill." Rice ran the steep climb every day after the season ended, which was 2.5 miles up.

"It taught me endurance," remarked Rice. "Being able to function when you're really tired." When all else fails, you find a way to dig a little deeper. So the final 800 metres made a lot of guys cry. It caused a number of men to vomit. That was part of my off-season routine."

Jerry ran The Hill to fulfil his aspirations and obtain his Super Bowl rings. Some players undoubtedly told him that running hills had nothing to do with football and that it didn't help a man improve his catching ability. They claimed this primarily because they didn't want to run hills because it was difficult, so by dismissing Jerry's method, they established an escape route for themselves. Jerry was convinced otherwise, therefore he performed it religiously. He outworked the competition and got three Super Bowl rings by running hills. Did he benefit from hill running? It certainly appeared to. He is the undisputed GOAT among NFL wide receivers.

When it comes to Jerry Rice, his former colleagues can attest to his passion.

"I don't think I've ever met anyone with a greater obsession with perfection than Jerry," former 49ers tight end Brent Jones remarked.

"He wanted to be flawless in every aspect of the game." He was tremendously motivated by it."

That is the mindset I bring with me into the woods. I am obsessed with the prospect of not being successful on a search. That is why I run on my own hill. I run because I believe it has assisted me in achieving my goals. And, like Jerry's detractors, lots of individuals have slammed me for thirty years and dismissed my instruction. They say running to prepare for bow season is a waste of time, but each year I find success. It could be a waste of time for some weak souls who don't have what it takes to work and sacrifice, or for those who don't prioritise hunting the way I do.

You must work hard and make sacrifices. To succeed, you must stand out. You have to decide what you want to be and what you want to excel at. You can't achieve 100 different things because excelling requires obsessiveness. So, if you're obsessed with business, you probably won't have time to be obsessed with archery. Because that is what is required. Obsession with being the best at one thing.

I'll give you an example.

We have high aspirations and expectations for our children as parents. The most important thing for me is that I've always wanted to set a good example for my children and show them what hard effort can achieve. I've told them over and over that I'm nothing exceptional. Tanner and Truett are more athletic than me, I've told them. I told Taryn she was smarter than I was. They are all far better individuals than I was when they were their age. So, if I've accomplished what I've accomplished, I've told them, you can accomplish even more. I want to show my children what it is to give your all.

Returning to the topic of fixation, if you're going to be excellent at one thing, you're generally not going to be great at anything else. From my perspective, I know I've fallen short in some areas because I've been obsessed with other things. Because I've been obsessed with bowhunting, I'm sure I wasn't the best father, spouse, or whatever. Spending $3,000 to go on an out-of-state hunt when you don't have the money and have a newborn baby at home, for example, is generally not a good idea. That is not being the best provider you can be since I prioritise my dream over being a provider for my family and those that rely on me. If you're being honest with yourself, as I have been, you'll realise you've fallen short. That is not a justification; it is simply being honest.

What we demand of our children isn't always in line with what we expect of ourselves. We push them and tell them, "You don't have to be the best; just give your best," even if many of us are merely going through the motions at work and in life. But I've always made a point of giving more and working more than others, and I've tried to instil that philosophy in my children.

"Listen, you guys aren't special," I told them all the time. "If you give what everyone else gives, you won't stand out." If you want to achieve anything, you'll have to contribute more. You must give more than everyone else."

That's always been my attitude, but as a parent, I've had my doubts. When my boys were younger, they would spend the night with their friends and return home with stories about the other fathers. Personally, I'd reply, "Well, he's teaching his son to be a pussy, basically." I wanted my children to be prepared for the crap we face in life, since life is a competition. You must make sacrifices if you want to succeed. So, while I may not have taught them certain things, I did educate them how to be tough. I was usually harsh with them, particularly the lads. I loved them, and they knew I loved them, but I'd never let them off the hook.

As I've gotten older, I've started to regret how I raised kids and what I said to them. Did I mess up these kids?

Tanner came in and informed us he was going to Army basic camp because he wanted to be an Army Ranger. I had an awful idea. Is it possible that my strange excessive approach to life has damaged this kid? Tanner was a sheriff's deputy in our town at the time, which is an excellent profession. He was earning $70,000 a year, and it is a respected, important field that could lead to a fulfilling career. I was pleased with his performance as a deputy and quite proud of him. But I had also warned them while they were growing up, "If you're average, you're a failure!" I had confessed to them that I had never meant to say that having an ordinary job and an average life meant you were a failure. I was mistaken. Nothing is wrong with that. We need people we can rely on for work like these. Regret was whispering in my ear.

Did I screw up my boys?

Tanner reassured me before leaving for basic training when I chatted with him. "No, Dad. It's just that I feel like I have more to offer the world than working at the jail for the next 25 years."

He is correct: Being a Ranger is a difficult job. Rangers are elite soldiers, but he's really good at it and a beast.

Trying to give life to this thinking of mine was perhaps the most difficult aspect of parenting my children.

"God, life is hard," I've told myself. "How come it feels so unfair and upsetting?"

I've learned the hard way that if you're weak in body and spirit, life will be that much more difficult. Knowing this meant I had to be tough on them.

Tanner was home on leave recently and was watching some of his old high school basketball tapes.

"Dad, you were correct! "I was so sluggish."

"No shit," I said.

"I never played defence."

"No kidding!"

He's twenty-seven now and can see it, but we used to have the most heated debates about effort back then. "You get on that ball," I was continually saying. "Be prepared!" But he refused to do it. On offence, he was fantastic; as a senior, he once scored 32 points in a half and was named All-State. So I thought in my mind what he could have accomplished if he had tried harder. Nonetheless, I would occasionally second-guess myself. Is it just me, or is he giving it his all?

Every day, I feel that if you're not giving your all, you're not truly honouring the gift of life. I don't want to merely survive. At the same time, I don't want to dismiss others who give their all in different ways, such as mothers who give it their all and believe that being the best means being the most nurturing and loving mother to their children. about the boys, I was more concerned about providing everything you had physically, but with Taryn, I've had to change. For her, it means aiming for greatness in scholastic and intellectual pursuits because that is where she shines. She is, in fact, smart, so in keeping with my revised expectations, I am attempting to persuade her to apply to Oxford University or another prestigious school of higher study. She has talent.

Truett recently completed his first 100-mile endurance foot race. He broke David Goggins' 24-hour pull-up record of 4,030 last year by doing 4,100. Achievements like this prompt me to think about how much being a father to my three lovely children has enhanced my life. I've failed as a parent numerous times and may have been overly harsh on my children in the belief that I was "preparing them" for the hardships that life would inevitably come their way. These reservations have been alleviated for a couple of reasons that have nothing to do with me. One, Tracey has shown unshakable motherly love and support when I've been too harsh or demanding, and two, our kids (who are no longer children; men and a perfect young girl) are tough, smart, and far more capable than most. Because of these factors, my mistakes as a father are less visible to others. They are obvious to me.

All of that being said, what I've always tried to do with "expectations" is to make sure that, while I expect a lot of others, it's not more than I expect of myself.

Make no excuses, give your all, show up when you're supposed to, speak your mind, admit your faults, think critically, and live a life worth remembering.

Something occurred to me as I was drafting the last few phrases. My children may better reflect these characteristics than I do. Maybe the teacher has turned into the student?

I persevere.

Everyone has different strengths; mine is the ability to persevere in the mountains. To put up with the agony, the pace, the frustration, everything. If I keep pushing, I will finally overcome whatever obstacle is preventing me from accomplishing my goal.

That makes me feel unstoppable. That makes me feel less like an impostor. This explains my obsession. Perhaps this explains why I am an example to others.

Many years ago, I resolved to work hard every day to become the finest bowhunter I could be. That is my life's purpose, along with taking care of my family. Everything I do revolves around this desire and aspiration.

Every day, I begin at 5:00 a.m. and end at 8:00 p.m.

I give it my all.

I am grateful for the gifts and opportunities that have been bestowed upon me.

I am enjoying the journey.

Steve Prefontaine was spot on. "To give anything less than your best is to sacrifice the gift."

That's exactly how I see it.

Bowhunting can be difficult. It's difficult and competitive. It can be really competitive. But so, too, can life.

Our life's passions, goals, and dreams can resemble the Dall sheep I arrowed with Roy in Alaska. Sometimes such dreams are bleeding and clutching to life on the edge of a precipice.

Life may be difficult and draining. We have suffered loss. A loved one or a family member, a job or a dream are all examples of such things. We are fighting our own demons and dependencies. We're all hit and battered down.

That is when we must make a decision.

Only you have the option of not hesitating.

Only you have the ability to continue moving.

Only you can climb over snow and ice, difficult footing, and steep, harsh terrain.

You're the only one who can eventually grip those horns and see if there's any life still in them.

You're going to have to battle for it. You're getting kicked. It can be difficult to hold on to hope. It's simple to give up.

Will your dream be dragged off the ledge?

Will you be able to stay alive?

Can you muster the courage to persevere?

Time stopped for a second when I grabbed the horns of the Dall sheep. My entire existence flashed before my eyes. I remembered everyone who meant a lot to me.

Is this the end?

I was clutching a 250-pound wild beast that, with one wrong move, could pull me over the precipice. I eventually pulled him up onto that small ledge, tied him up, and kept him there.

I took a deep breath and looked down the mountain.

I made it. I'm going to make it through this.

I praised God for another day to see those I care about. I walked away from that mountain with a prize on my back.

Looking back, it was a dubious move to try to keep him inches away from certain death, but this was my sheep. I had waited my entire life for that moment. I had a dream in my hands, and I wasn't about to give it up for anything.

What is the cliff you're standing next to, and what will keep you from tumbling over it?

What dream do you have that you will not give up on?

My accomplishment on Pioneer Peak was one I never imagined I'd attain. It also serves as a reminder of what I frequently say...

Anyone can do it if I can. But you'll have to work for it.

You'll have to put up with it.

AFTERWORD

My entire life, I was obsessed with discovering the toughest men on the earth. I looked for them in the most arduous positions in the military as well as the endurance competitions in which I competed. I had no notion that a random contact would lead me to such a barbarian. Only one man sticks out among the numerous toughest and fiercest individuals I've trained with. Cameron Hanes is the one. If any of you know who I am, you will understand that I am not saying this to promote a section in his book; rather, I am saying it because it is true. On a daily basis, he epitomises what it means to strive beyond human capabilities. That is what distinguishes him. He constantly challenges and pushes his limits on a daily basis. In doing so, he has and continues to inspire millions. As we run 6-minute miles on a 20-mile training run, he encourages every runner and biker who passes us with his famous phrase, "Keep Hammering."

His thinking is such that he does not simply desire to be a hunter. He doesn't want to be just a runner. He doesn't want to only lift weights. He strives to perform everything at the greatest level possible and is constantly on the lookout for the best in order to better himself.

This individual is really simple to misread. When someone is driven to be the best, they are often misunderstood because he forces you to look in the mirror. Because of how hard he works, he makes you examine yourself to see what you might be doing. He works himself to exhaustion on a daily basis in order to show others what is possible. Cameron is a traditional leader who leads by example rather than by speaking. That is evident by his incredible family. His children show a work ethic and discipline that is uncommon these days, all of which they learnt by watching their father pour every ounce of his spirit into being his best. I used to assume I was alone out here, never imagining that someone else was working as hard as I did. I'm now aware of another. We don't talk about it when I see Cameron Hanes, but I know we're both attempting to break the other one. Cameron conducted a background check on me in January 2021. If you don't know what a spot-check is, it's when a friend contacts you out of nowhere and informs you he or she is coming into town. The goal is to catch you when you slip. I can't ever slip because I know there is a Cameron Hanes out there who has my number.

When Can called to say he was coming to town and wanted to go for an "easy, light run" and lift some weights, I knew exactly what he meant. It meant a long, hard run followed by a punishing ass weight training. Knowing that, I decided it was time to break Cam. He was coming to my home soil, you see. I knew the route, the distance, all of the variables, and the pace. So we met at Las Vegas' M Hotel, and I took him on one of my normal outings. My girl was with me, so I believe he assumed we were heading out for a casual night. He had no idea my gal could throw down.

We were approximately 7 miles into the run when my girlfriend decided she could only go 14 miles, so she turned back and we continued on. This was where my strategy would be put into action. The plan was to take Cameron out three more miles, giving us a total of ten miles before turning around.

I know you can't feel the descent as you set out, but Cam doesn't. My plan was to break him going back 10 miles uphill. I started at a 6:30/mile pace at the turnaround. I could see the incline was bothering him because he began to fade away from my left shoulder and stopped talking. We had nine kilometres to go, and they were all uphill. As we approached mile 15, I could tell he was exhausted, as was I. My plan to break Cameron Hanes was starting to unravel. The more I attempted to break him, the faster he became. Cam was no longer a step behind, but a step ahead of me before I realised it. Cameron was now following me around. The tables had shifted.

– David Goggins

June 2021

The contents of this book may not be copied, reproduced or transmitted without the express written permission of the author or publisher. Under no circumstances will the publisher or author be responsible or liable for any damages, compensation or monetary loss arising from the information contained in this book, whether directly or indirectly. .

Disclaimer Notice:

Although the author and publisher have made every effort to ensure the accuracy and completeness of the content, they do not, however, make any representations or warranties as to the accuracy, completeness, or reliability of the content. , suitability or availability of the information, products, services or related graphics contained in the book for any purpose. Readers are solely responsible for their use of the information contained in this book

Every effort has been made to make this book possible. If any omission or error has occurred unintentionally, the author and publisher will be happy to acknowledge it in upcoming versions.

Copyright © 2023
All rights reserved.

Printed in Great Britain
by Amazon